MW01290927

Chakras for Beginners:

A Complete Guide to Balance Chakras and Healing Yourself with Crystals and Meditation for Health and Positive Energy.

Lisle Kepler

Table of Contents

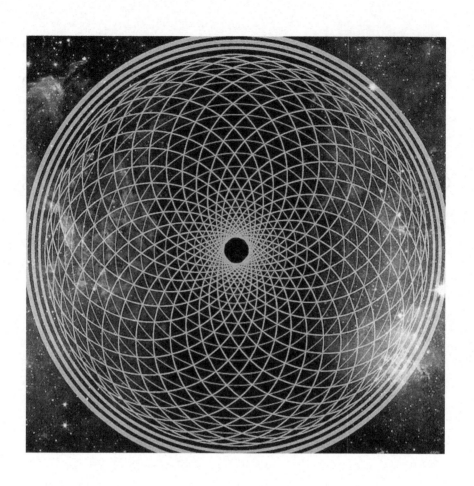

Introduction

Welcome to *Chakras for Beginners: A Complete Guide to Balance Chakras and Healing Yourself with Crystals and Meditation for Health and Positive Energy!* I am so happy that you have chosen to learn more about the power of your chakra system and how to work with healing yourself for a happier, healthier and more positive life.

How much do you already know about your chakras? If you are reading this book, then you probably have a lot of questions that need answering and you are in luck because this guide is here to show you the way. There are so many wonderful ways that you can explore not just your physical health, but your emotional and mental health as well.

The history of the chakras is ancient and comes from another culture that accurately described the essence of our "subtle bodies". If you practice yoga, you might know a thing or two about these concepts because the same culture that invented yoga practices, also wrote about our chakras and how they work. In this book, you will learn more about the history of how chakras came to be known, and how we are only just learning about the science behind them in our western culture.

You will learn about the individual chakras that make up the main chakra system, as well as the additional chakras that can exist at other points in your body. It is important that as you learn more about each of these "energy centers" that you know how they can impact your overall health. This guide will give you explanations for how your chakras can become imbalanced or blocked and why that can cause physical, emotional, and mental side effects.

You want to know how to heal those blocks and imbalances and this book is the perfect guide for beginners to get acquainted with a variety of ways to heal the energy of your system. Some of the methods you will learn include yoga, meditation, mindfulness and how to use crystals for chakra cleansing and why they are so very important to the process.

So much of our life journey is supported by going to see the doctor or the therapist to coach us through our healing and our progress; but what if you could take charge of so much of that and compliment your healthcare practices by understanding your own unique energy flow and how it has such an impact on your physical health and your emotional well-being? Well, this book explains that whole process and how healing your chakras might help you need the doctor less and your own healing medicine more.

Chakras for Beginners will help you attain all of the information that you need to get started on your own personal healing journey. There are so many layers to the self and wanting to discover more about your unique life-force and vibrational frequency is a perfect beginning to tapping into the 'YOU' you have always wanted to be. Experience is not necessary or required in the field of chakra healing in order to reap the benefits of connecting to your energetic centers.

You and your body know so much more than you might think, and listening to the communication your body sends to you through your chakras is part of the pleasure of uniting with your own healing process. I hope you will enjoy taking this journey together and if you are ready to explore the intricacies of your beautiful light and vibration, then let's begin the colorful road trip through the chakras and give you all the resources you need to balance, cleanse, rejuvenate and live the life of abundance you have always wanted!

Chapter 1: History of Chakras

There is a long and intricate history behind the energy centers, or nadis, that are assigned the name chakra. There term itself is a Sanskrit word that means "wheel", and describes the nature and form of the energy that rests inside of your body as 7 main vortexes up through your spine.

The question is, where did this knowledge and philosophy come from in the first place. The Hindu religion of India has a long history of certain types of health practice mixed with spiritual belief. In India, yoga has been one of the greatest techniques to spread across the world and become a mainstream element of cultural self-care, wholeness, and enlightenment. It is an exercise that bridges the world between the physical and spiritual health of a person and interestingly enough, chakras come from the same philosophy and practice.

Somewhere between 1500 and 500 BC, the Vedas were written in Sanskrit in Eastern cultures to explain and describe certain philosophies and practices of the Hindu religions. There are many different studies included in the Vedas and other references known as the Upanishads. Within these texts, the information describing the energy wheels, or chakras, was found and contributed to the overall philosophy that all individuals are made up of different elements.

The most commonly understood elements in Western culture pertain to the physical body, which consists of your muscles, bones, tissues and various organ systems, and your emotional/mental body, which consists of your thoughts, feelings and mental experiences and knowledge.

Unlike Western medicine and spirituality, Eastern practices were incorporating a whole-body connection into their practices, long before Yoga was being practiced in every city in America. The reality of the mind-body-spirit connection has been studied and linked to everyone's essential nature through a variety of skills, techniques, practices and methods, yoga being the most commonly practiced and known.

With every energy center in your body there is a quality and characteristic that links to an emotional and physical part of the self. For centuries, Indian culture has been utilizing this knowledge to promote long life, happiness and health, as well as a connection to their Gods and divine connection to Source. The reality is that there have always been chakras, but they are only referred to in this language because this culture was the first known to describe it in a language and write it down as information to be studied.

Prior to the existence of the Vedas, the information about chakras was passed down through oral teaching and was taught to students who could change their energy for religious and healing purposes. It has grown in popularity in the recent years and came into the West around the time of the 1960's when certain Gurus were bringing their knowledge to other cultures to share their wisdom and expand the global consciousness.

To be clear, the history of the chakras might be founded and explained in the religious texts of the Hindu culture, however, learning what the chakras are and what they do is not a religious practice. You could ascertain that it has something to do with spirituality, only because of its connection to the "spiritual" energy of the self, or as some descriptions would call it, the "subtle body".

There are other cultures that have described the same chakra energy with different terminology and theory of practice. Take the example of Qi (chi) in Chinese medicine. The concept of Qi relates to the meridians of the body, or energetic channels in which the life-force energy (Qi) will flow through and provide a balance and general good health. If the channels are blocked or influenced in negative ways, the Qi must regain proper function and flow.

Chines medicine is a large part if the culture that ascribes this energetic life-force to how all people are physically, mentally, and emotionally treated for their ailments. The practice of Tai-chi is all about harnessing the flow of Qi so that it remains in a healthy rhythm.

Another consideration of Chinese medicine is acupuncture. This practice of placing small needles into tiny energy portals throughout the meridians of the body are intended to help regain a balanced flow to the energy of the body so that normal body function can be attained.

Other remote cultures have utilized these concepts in their religious rituals and witch-doctor, or shaman, healing work and they have never become mainstream ideologies of healing practice. To gain a deeper understanding of the chakras, it is important to visit the other cultures that have described this concept, not just the origin of the name for it, as in the Hindu texts that first used the word chakra.

Connecting to the history helps to understand the purpose of these centers of energy and life-force. They have always existed in our human forms and we have only learned how to explain and describe them in the recent past. There are plenty of new advances in science and culture that seek to explain the concept of chakras from a more rational and realistic point of view that is not related to any kind of religious or spiritual practice, but the fact of the matter is that all of these studies and research are capable of missing the finer points of the chakra system and why it can be helpful to acknowledge them from a more spiritual point of view.

The beliefs that surround the chakras have a great deal to do with the experience of becoming enlightened. One of the main purposes of healing, opening and maintain a balance within your chakra system id to transcend human drama and life challenges to become a whole being of high vibrational frequency that has the capacity to connect with "Source".

There is no religion in this book, but we will talk about the concept of the Universal consciousness and the reality of "divine energy" and what that means to the chakra system. Energy is universal and we are all made of energy. The quality of your energy, according to the Vedas and other texts, will improve your capacity to align with your highest self and highest purpose as an individual in the greater wholeness of all things on Earth and beyond.

If you have ever practiced yoga, you may have learned some of these ideas before. To awaken your whole being to the concept of enlightenment requires the energetic work of letting go of limiting beliefs, outdated thought patterns, karmic patterns and behaviors that prevent you from transcending and evolving as a person and as a species.

Within the history of the chakras lies the deeper meaning of life and the "why we are all here" question. Everyone who asks that question is looking for the answer as an individual about to go on a quest to find the truth behind their purpose and identity. The world outside of ourselves informs everything we do, every decision we make, how we express our knowledge, or joys and concerns, our happiness and sorrow.

When we lack the knowledge to improve ourselves and we seek outside of ourselves for the answers, we come up short. The reason is because the answers are, and always have been, within the energy of the self. When the Vedas appeared and gave context to these realities, it began a long story with certain cultures about the answers to enlightenment and the truth of our natures.

All of your current trust in these systems is largely based on belief and for many, that is not enough to support and idea of reality. So many Westerners will see only medical assistance to "heal" their issues, without allowing for the possibility that they are working on only ¼ of their whole being.

Other cultures have successfully proven that the concept of these energy planes is as vital to health and wholeness as just your physical well-being is, and that we all benefit on a deeper level when we address the system as a whole, instead of in parts.

The energy centers of your body are called chakras because of their name being originally set down by only one culture, but they are always present in all people, no matter what culture you are from. If you want, you can make up your own name to describe them. You don't have to call them chakras because that is just their historical name based on who described them to begin with.

When you begin to learn more about them, you will understand that the chakras are universal and belong to all culture and all identities, but that not all people are confident in their existence. Because of the considerably esoteric, or metaphysical, quality of their existence, it is hard for everyone to believe in what they are and how they work.

Besides their invisible nature, they are actually incredibly capable of being detected, either through your own feelings, or through the measurement of vibrational frequency. All of us are comprised of energy, as well as physical matter, and our energy has frequency. The best way to understand the chakras, especially if you are a beginner to the subject, is to look to the science of how they work and why it is possible to heal yourself through your energy.

The following chapter will go into greater detail about how your chakra system is really all about frequency and that you can measure the energy of chakras with some incredibly simple tools.

Chapter 2: The Science of Chakras

How much do you know about energy? There is a whole science behind energy and the way that it performs. If you have ever taken a basic science class in your elementary or high school, then you have some idea of how chakras work. To be specific, energy is a force that exists all around us. When you your heart starts beating rapidly after playing a rousing game of soccer, you are expelling a great deal more energy than you were before you started running around the field.

If you have ever felt static electricity, when your hair stands on end, that's energy. The way magnets push each other apart when they are facing opposite poles; that's energy, too! Everyone and everything have some form of energy that exists and it has a lot to do with what we are made of.

There are the simple elements as you might have heard of them: earth, air, fire and water. What about the entire Periodic Table of elements? Every element on the Periodic Table has some measure of energy. Typically, in science, weight and mass are the aspects that will give something a certain form of energy and all of the elements have this. These elements report what they are through their physical make up and the way that they energetically exist in the world. Sometimes, when you mix certain elements together, you create new forms of energy, by making and forming new elements.

Other changes will occur in energy when it changes from liquid to solid, or gas. This type of energy change is something to consider when you think about how chakras work inside of you. Although your chakra energy will never become a solid in your body, it can cause a frequency to alter your energetic vibration in certain organ systems that can cause stiffness, tightness, or achiness.

Everyone around you is carrying their own frequency of energy. So, then let's talk about frequency. Why are some frequencies different than others and why are some positive or negative? If you were to take the feeling of happiness and measure it, what kind of frequency do you think it would have? Positive or negative? If you chose positive, you would be right. The frequencies associated with positive and negative frequencies are often referred to as being high or low vibration.

Frequencies are vibrations of energy and some resonate at a higher frequency than others. Take for example the feeling of happiness again. Happiness is an emotion or state of being that allows you to feel blissful, elated, jovial, and in good spirits. This energy is strong and even contagious. It has the power to make your whole life feel great and it is what so many of us are looking forward to maintaining on a regular basis.

This high frequency of vibration allows your energy to have a higher elevation in your mind and subsequently in your whole body and being. It has always been this way, since humankind first understood the word 'smile'.

Consider the other end of the spectrum and take sadness. What does sadness feel like as an energy? Low, uncomfortable, tragic, negative. If you were to ask yourself how often you have that emotion or feeling allowing for the concept of energy to inform your words, you might simply say that your vibrational frequency is lower than usual and all I need to do to adjust my frequency is to change my energy to a higher vibration.

Assessment of your own energy, in addition to your body, mind and emotions, is part of what the chakra healing method is all about. Your chakras are always influencing the system of your whole being and as it happens, even when you are having a sore throat, your chakra energy is involved and influenced by your sickness.

You don't have to be a science expert to get this concept. It really boils down to understanding that the physical matter of your body is always affected by the energy of your chakras, the same way that the energy of your thoughts and feelings is always impacted by the energy of your chakras and what you take in on a daily level.

Now that you have a basic idea of the science behind chakras, let's take it a step further. How is your energy affected throughout the day by all of the other energies you come into contact with? Here is a good example of what that might look like:

Perhaps you are in a great mood today and you are feeling on top of your game. You got up early, did your exercise routine, skipped the coffee and had a healthy smoothie, before hopping in your car and heading to work, whistling. Out of nowhere the sky darkens and the rain comes pouring down and you are stuck in traffic. You will be late to work and you can't be late again or you will get in trouble. The pressure is building. As you are pulling into the parking garage, another driver takes the last available spot, forcing you to find street parking and run inside in the rain, getting drenched from head to toe. You are late for the meeting and soaking wet. So much for a blissful Monday.

So, what on Earth does energy and chakras have to do with this scenario? In all seriousness, many of us are in the habit of letting our moods be dictated by outside occurrences, which inevitably lead to a change in energetic frequency. Life is always coming at you and there are theories that if you just smile through it then it will go away and be okay and you will make the most out of everything, even when it means being 45 minutes late and wet to an important meeting with the boss.

The reality is that even if you are able to stay in a relatively pleasant mood under these conditions, your energy will still be impacted on a deeper level because of the overall energy and vibration of your experiences. You may be able to stay calm throughout, but how about all of the other people surrounding you in traffic who are radiating frustration and anger at the rain, who is never to blame for coming down. The energy of everything around you will have an influence on your experience and it will absorb into your own frequency, shifting it slightly in one way or another.

Your body may not be conscious of this, nor will your mind be, however your "subtle body" is incredibly receptive and is always engaged in what is going on around it. Let's take another example of how your frequency can be altered in your daily life:

You just broke up with your partner because they were telling you that they wanted to see someone else and that they had already started dating them, leaving you feeling angry and confused about how long they might have been cheating. You are always kind and offered so much affection and love to your mate that you can't possibly see why they would want to date anyone else, or how they managed to put on such an act of wanting to stay close to you for so long, whilst lying to your face about another partner. You are ready to answer all of these questions and suddenly you get a phone call from your ex who has already decided that the other person isn't a good fit and that they want to come back to you. You are confused and conflicted because of how they acted, but you ask for them to stay with you because you want to be back together.

Two months later, they are doing it again and this time, you catch all of the signals of their cheating. How? Because your energy has shifted to know and understand that they are not at the same frequency anymore. You can tell when their energy changes because you are hyper sensitive to your partner's energy after the traumatic relationship drama you just endured. You can energetically sense that they have gone out with someone else effecting their frequency and their energy to the point that it becomes noticeable to you.

Energy plays such a huge role in our experiences. Most of us are taught when we are young that life is only a matter of your body and your mind and sometimes how you process your feelings, and even that is a stretch for some people. So much of our definition of life revolves around what your body says, what your mind thinks, and what your heart feels, but how about how your energy influences all three of those factors simultaneously?

Bridging the gap between the physical and the ethereal is hard to do in the scientific community. The esoteric community has no problem with associating the concept of chakras to the science of the whole body and how it functions on a physical, emotional and mental level. That is what the methods described in yoga practices are all about: incorporating the entire system, not just attaching to one side of it to resolve and issue.

For those who have to have a more rational explanation for the science of chakras all you need to know is that they are all energetic frequencies. Each one has its own range of frequency, too. They don't vibrate at the same rate, which means they all have different qualities and characteristics associate with them. In order to understand this, you will have to meet the chakras themselves and get to know why the energetic frequency of each one is so different.

In the next chapter you will learn more about the seven, main chakras, and how they are an influence to everything about your body, mind and feelings. In addition, you will learn about some of the less commonly known chakras that play an important role in all matters "energy".

Chapter 3: The Chakra System

Our chakra system is not open to view with the naked eye. There are those who are capable of seeing the auric field with their vision, which will usually be represented by a color. This color that is present as "aura" is actually a reflection of the chakra energy of the body. If you have ever had a photograph taken of your auras, or seen someone else's aura photo, you can see an ethereal wisp of color coming off of the person's body.

This is a lot like what the chakra areas of the body look like as they radiate frequency inside of you. It has been proven that each frequency of energy on a certain spectrum is associated with a specific color. The reason for this pertains to the light spectrum.

Have you ever seen a prism? When you hold it up to the light and rotate it in your hand, there are colors that shift inside of it and they are all the colors of the rainbow. Sometimes, when the sunlight catches the prism at the right angle, it will cast a rainbow-colored reflection onto the wall or ceiling. The point of knowing this is to understand that color is light and frequency, and so when dealing with the energies of your own chakra system, you can connect it to the reality of having your own light frequency within.

As you learned in the previous chapter, each chakra has its own frequency and that they are not all vibrating at the same rate. This is why each chakra is known to have a different color and also how the science behind energy can support this reality. We are made of light, just like the prism casting the rainbow on the wall.

When you ask yourself what all of this means, what is the first thing that pops into your head? How likely are you to see your own light and feel your own vibration? Is that something you are prepared to do, knowing what you know now about how your internal vibrational frequencies are? Can you picture them in your mind right now?

Try this exercise: close your eyes and see your body in your mind's eye. Project the image of yourself in your internal eye so that you can see the detail of yourself. Now, at the base of your spine, at the tail end of your coccyx, see an orb of reddish colored light. Ask it what it does and why it is there. It is okay of you don't get a response.

Now, move up to your pelvis, just below your navel and picture an orb of orange colored light. How big is it? Is it moving at all? Spinning? Can you feel any energy here while you picture this orangey orb?

Moving up your spinal column some more, see just above your belly button and below your sternum, a yellow orb of light.

How does it feel here? What kind of energy can you notice if any?

Continue up into your chest to your heart space. Here you will picture a green-glowing orb of light. Are you noticing any energy when you focus here? How are you feeling when you settle on this area?

Following the spine up to the neck, right at the base of the throat, see a bluish colored orb of light. What kind of energy is here? Are you able to see the orb well in this area? Can you picture its color?

Continuing further up, focus on the area just above and between your eye brows. Your third eye is here and it is how you have been picturing this entire meditation in your head. Picture an indigo colored orb of light here and notice any energy that you may have when you focus on this space. How does it feel?

Lastly, continue your view up to the top of your head and see a violet orb of light sitting just barely outside the top of your skull. What does it feel like in this place? Are you able to access an energy or vibration when you concentrate on this orb of energetic light?

Now, zoom out a little and see your whole body and every orb of colorful light that exists inside of you. You have just taken a tour through your own chakra system and can now see how it looks from within. You may not be able to see it clearly with your eyes open, but you can certainly picture these bodies of energy with your eyes closed and your third eye focused on what is under your surface.

Take a moment to reflect on this energy. Question the energies that you may have felt as you rose up your spine picturing each, colorful orb of light. What sensations were there, if any? Did you have any thoughts or feelings creep in with certain placements? Were you able to clearly see them, or did they look faint and hardly noticeable? Do you like asking these questions?

If you do, then this chapter will be a fun one for you because it is all about the chakra system and what each of the seven main chakras represent to your mind, body and heart and how each one's characteristics can have an obvious impact on your general health and wellness.

The Seven Main Chakras

To go through the seven main chakras is to do what you have just done in the visualization meditation. You can now "see" where they are and how they might look. They are "wheels" of energy along your spine, from tailbone to crown, and each has its own position of energetic power.

Each one may have its own unique qualities, however, they all work together as a team to support your energy overall. When you have blockages or imbalances, other energy wheels will compensate and either become to excessive in energy, or too deficient as a result. That is part of why it is so important to create the balance and clear the system of any wounds, pain, trauma, insecurities, fears, and repressed emotions.

When you are dealing with your own work on your chakras, you will have to be the judge of these "senses" or feelings about what you are not letting go of, or how you are projecting certain feelings through a certain chakra. This helps you to practice self-awareness so that you can be ready to gain more energetic life-force in your own system. It is a part of the healing journey to connect with yourself on every level and the chakra system can help you identify where you are the most blocked, uncomfortable and insecure.

As you read through this chapter, you will discover more information about the wonderful world of your energy centers and how each will have a specific impact on your entire physical, mental, emotional and spiritual self. This section will go into greater depth about the seven main chakras, the ones you pictured in your meditation, before going into what the Twelve Chakra system looks like.

The Root Chakra

Let's start at the base and work our way up, as you did in your visualization. The root chakra is located at the base of the spine is the color red. It has an energy of rootedness and groundedness and involves the quality of security and survival. It is your most basic and primitive need.

For many people, this chakra has the answers to all insecurities, doubts, fears and ancestral patterns that are repeated through the generations. It has a way of holding onto a lot of anxiety about wealth and financial security, as well as feelings of worthiness to have what you want and need to survive.

All of the energy of this chakra is very primal and supports the entire system when in a healthy flow and balanced vibration. It has the opportunity of awakening your kundalini energy, which is considered a more advanced form of chakra healing work that begins the whole-body alignment that leads to enlightenment.

Basically, this means that your root chakra is the beginning of soul awakening and the kundalini (ancient Sanskrit word to describe your coiled up, dormant life-force) is stored here until you are ready to "awaken" to your power.

The root chakra is also associated with the quality of the Earth element and as such has a very grounded energy. As it is named "root", think of the roots of a tree digging down into the soil. The root chakra helps you to plant your roots so that you can feel stable and secure in all areas of your life.

The Sacral Chakra

Next in line up the spine is the second chakra. It is called the sacral chakra because it vibrates at the point of the spine where your sacrum is and has a lot to do with the energy of this area of your body. Inside of your body at this point is where a human being's sex organs are located. It is a part of us all to have passion and desire and that is the energy of this area.

When you think about the correlation to the placement, and the location of the uterus, ovaries and close proximity of the male gonads, then you can understand why this vibrational frequency would be associated with sexuality.

It is not all about sex in this chakra, however. There is the energy of creation, and not just of new life, like when you procreate to have children; it is about the creativity that exists in all life and everything that we do as people. We all have this creative energy and for some it is more productive and proactive than in others.

The sacral chakra is about creative life-force, as well as passion and desire. It has a great deal to do with our emotions and is connected to the element, Water. Emotions are watery and that is why there is a link to these energetic qualities. Many people assume that there is no need to have any creativity in their lives, or that they are simply not a creative person, when in reality, all of us is a creative life spark and sometimes a lack of creativity can come from an emotional block in the second chakra.

This chakra is also about intimacy and person-to-person connection, whether it is sexual, platonic, or familial. You don't have to associate this chakra with the actual act of sex; it is more about your right to feel things in your life, and that includes other people you are romantically involved with.

This chakra is all about feelings, creative power, connection and intimacy with others, passion and desire and will be a powerful source of love, joy and creative power.

The Solar Plexus Chakra

Moving right on up the spine to the area just above your navel, we come to the solar plexus, or 3rd chakra, and it has a yellow color. Think of a bright sun glowing at this center of your body. It makes sense, since this chakra pertains to the element of Fire. This is the spot most commonly associated with the self and the power of "I am". It is an action-oriented center and has a lot to do with your personal power and how you achieve what you want in your life.

When you are happy in your life path and you are accomplishing all of your daily goals and life plans, this chakra is doing well and open energetically. It has a placement in your body that is all about energy. This is your vitality and strength. It is the location of where you digest food and convert it into energy for your whole body to use. It is how you work out your force and direct yourself forward in life.

There are a lot of possibilities for this chakra to become blocked, excessive, deficient or stagnant. Even though it is not numerically in the center of the chakra system, it is physically located between the upper and lower body. As you get into the heart chakra and move up through the crown, you are dealing with a different frequency of energies.

Some people will say that the heart is the bridge between the upper and lower chakras and that is a valid argument;

however, it is the solar plexus chakra assessment that shows you how well you take action with all of the other chakra energies in your system. Here is where the life force energy of your whole system can get very blocked, stagnant, or stuck.

You will notice this chakra allows you to feel vibrant, action-oriented, ambitious, driven, excited, vital and full of personal power to accomplish your goals and life plans. It is your will power and it is your identity expressing itself to the world.

The Heart Chakra

Oh, the heart, the glorious heart. The 4th chakra is so named because of its location, just as with all of the other chakras, and is green in color. It has the position of being in the center of your chest as it is associated with the organ of love. Love is actually the energetic frequency of this chakra. While the sacral chakra is about passion and connection, the heart chakra is more about all forms of love, from platonic to romantic, to self-love and love for all humankind and the whole Universe. It is connected to the element of Air, just as love is whimsical and changeful.

The love chakra is about how you experience love, how you give it and how you receive it. It has everything to do with your compassion and empathy for yourself and for other people, too. When you are here, you know what it feels like to be hurt by love, to feel the intoxication of love, and to be overly giving of it, without receiving anything for it in return.

Most of us are looking for love and it has a very strong power. As we are all looking for it, we have also all likely been wounded by it at one point or another. This chakra is talking about how it feels to give what you want and ask for it in return. It is your right to know love in all its forms. To many people, it can be the most important quality of life and has been revered throughout the ages as the reason for living.

When you are working with this energy, you may notice that there are a lot of blocks and dissonant frequencies because of how much we actually store in our hearts. So much of our fears that we won't be loved for who we are will come from this place. One of the greatest life lessons is how to love yourself unconditionally for who you are and for many that journey can be a real challenge. Isolating it in the heart chakra allows you to begin to ask the questions about how to love yourself more effectively, and it will always lead you toward the understanding of where else it manifests in your chakra system.

The heart is your bridge to the energy love. It has to do with every kind of love, not just romance, and seeks to bring harmony and balance to every relationship and experience with yourself and others.

The Throat Chakra

Up into the neck and at the location where the throat meets the clavicles, is the 5th chakra. The throat chakra is a bluish hue and exists in the location of your voice. Not surprisingly, it is the chakra of communication and is connected to the element of Sound. Sound is how you breathe life into your self-expression and ask it to come forward in a language we can all understand.

The act of speaking brings the energy of your thoughts, feelings, power, passion and security in yourself into the world through the vibration of your vocal cords. No other chakra expresses itself the way that the throat chakra does and as such, it holds a special place in the system. The throat chakra is the communicator for all of the other chakras and brings the knowledge of each energy to the surface to be heard.

The way we talk about ourselves, our lives, our beliefs and our emotions, all come through this energy center and so it is important to regard it as being a center for truth. When you have a difficult time communicating with other people, or yourself, you may have difficulty expressing how you truly feel, or what you really think, resulting in a lack of self-confidence and honest expression of self.

Our throat chakras reveal our self-mastery and our ability to witness and hear others as they communicate their own unique and divine power. The seat of communication is the ambassador for your whole energy system and will determine what you communicate to the world around you.

The Brow Chakra

Next in line along the chakra trail is the 6th chakra. The brow chakra is indigo and connects to the element of light. When you close your eyes and you picture something in your mind's eye, you can make out an image of light in this part of your mind. This energy center is commonly referred to as your third eye and it is the place where your sixth sense resides.

What is the sixth sense? This describes that part of every person connected to intuition, inner wisdom and even clairvoyance and psychic ability. Not all people believe that they have this kind of power, and yet the third eye would tell you otherwise. When your brow chakra has an ability to vibrate at its unblocked frequency, you can connect more to this aspect of yourself.

For a majority of people, there are significant blocks here and it can take years of energy healing work to become more enlightened and open in this part of the chakra system. People will often have beliefs and ideas that will confuse or distort their relationship to their "higher knowing", and so they may never truly become "awakened" in this energy center.

Remember when you practiced a visualization at the beginning of this chapter, to visually walk through each chakra and picture it in your mind? You were doing that in your third eye. It is your center for creative visualization and astral projection and it is how you can truly "see" what is beyond the third dimensional reality. That is the sixth sense.

Your third eye is your power to "see" and has everything to do with your innate wisdom, your ability to look beyond what is really in front of you, and how you explore and experience your intuitive powers and abilities.

The Crown Chakra

Finally, at the very tippy top of your head is the 7th, and final of the main chakras. The crown chakra is violet and happens to exist as your gateway to connect to the divine. The placement of the crown chakra is very close to the brow and they are there together to create a connection to what many will refer to as "Source" energy. Source is not a religious energy or affiliation and is meant to describe the energy of all things in the Universe, and so we will not put a name on it, such as God, or Allah. It is whatever you believe in or practice. The crown chakra is where the Universal life force energy pours into you and allows for the transcendence of time, space, and human drama to become an enlightened being.

The crown is connected to the element of Thought. Thought is an energy, just as much as anything else, and our thoughts create realities. The journey to awakening your crown chakra takes time and has a lot to do with how you clear and rebalance your other, lower chakras. This is how you get to the point of feeling truly awakened to your total power and purpose so that you can live as a whole being.

Not all people want to take their healing experience that far and there is a reason: enlightenment can be a difficult road and an arduous journey. It requires a willingness to sacrifice your entire life as you know it to become more awake to the whole existence of everything around you. For some, that can be too big a price and the more affordable goal is to just feel grounded and balanced.

The crown chakra asks for more from you and desires your connection to source and the wonderful world of all-things energy and the divinity of the Universe. This chakra is about transcendence, enlightenment, wholeness, universal truth, and the collective consciousness.

The Whole Balance

The seven main chakras are individuals. They are distinctly different and have their own personalities and attributes. When you look at them as individuals, you might be able to see how one might be stronger or more open than others, in your own system, and here is where it gets fun. Now, you can start asking why you feel so strongly in one part of your energy system, but diminished or deficient in another.

As you begin to explore your chakras, you get to be your own energy detective and solve the mystery of what is out of balance, remembering all of the qualities each one expresses and how that is involved in your daily life experiences.

When you get better acquainted with your own chakra system, it will become more obvious and you will be better able to intuit the direction your healing journey wants to go. As you gain trust in yourself and your energy work, you will know more about the dynamics each one plays in the greater whole.

The idea is to create a balance between all of the chakras so that they can exist in harmony and flow well. Think of a river flowing. The water pushes forward in a direction and moves on its journey that way. What if a dam starts to form? Driftwood starts to build up over time until the water won't flow freely anymore in several spots in the river, causing algae to build up and stagnation in the water.

It is your journey to find where the dams are blocking your flowing river so that you can remove the obstacles and refresh your energy flow. Here are the places you can go forward on this journey with a whole and balanced chakra system:

- Abundance and joy on a regular basis

- Lack of fear about your life choices

- Direction, focus and ambition about your life goals and dreams

- Attitude of gratitude everyday

- Physical/ emotional/ mental/ spiritual well-being

- Drama-free lifestyle and relationships

- Heartfelt appreciation of the self and others

- Strong sense of self-worth and confidence

- Past pains, traumas and wounds resolved, healed and forgiven

- Expressive and communicative nature and quality of life

- Powerful creative energy, passion and desire for joy and happiness

These are just some of the ways a balanced chakra system can affect your life. Your wholeness doesn't just depend on your physical health and your mental state. Both of those things are connected to your energy centers and your whole energy system. They are all always working together and the key to a healthy and abundant life is balance of the chakras.

The Twelve Chakra system

But wait, there's more! There are not just seven chakras to contend with; there are more subtle chakras all over your body. If you remember, in the first chapter about the history of chakras, reference was made to the concept of energy flow in relationship to acupuncture. Meridians are the channels in the body where Chinese medicine believes your Qi, or life-force energy flows. All of the needle placement points are actually tiny chakra centers that when stimulated with the point of the needle are able to rebalance and refresh a healthier flow of energy throughout the body.

By this estimation and theory, there are hundreds of these energy center in the body. In general, however, when working with your own chakras, you will mostly deal with the seven main chakras. Outside of that, there are a few more, larger chakra points in the body that have a huge impact on your overall energy.

The five additional chakras in your body that make a twelve-point chakra system are as follows:

- 2 chakras in the hands- one in each palm

- 2 chakras on the feet- one in each sole

- 1 chakra reaching out of the top of the head above the crown.

These additional five chakras are important to know about as much as any other energy center in the body, however, they are supportive to the rest of the system and will not hold onto energy in the same way that the seven main chakras will.

They are actually more like receivers. These chakras are gateways to the rest of your energy and are also transmitters of energy as well. Have you ever heard of the healing art known as Reiki? Reiki is a traditional Japanese healing technique that supports the rebalancing and energetic healing of the chakra system. A Reiki practitioner becomes attuned to heling these energies and will perform an energetic transformation of the chakra energies through the palm chakras, by moving and removing unwanted, stagnate, or stuck energies within the chakras.

A Reiki practioner learns how to take away, but not absorb someone's energy that they are working with through their hand chakras. The chakra centers in the soles of the feet are also receiving information while you are standing on the ground, lying on your back, or doing various other activities, but are not typically used in Reiki sessions, or for healing purposes.

Other ways that you are using your hand chakras are infinite: shaking someone's hand and getting a "feeling" about them; picking up an object at an antique store and "sensing" where it came from; feeling your child's forehead when they have a fever; picking out produce at the grocery store. Our hand chakras are aligning with everything that we touch.

Your feet are where you ground and how you walk through this world. Your ability to sense the world around you through your feet is very impactful and has an ability to connect you with things that you might not mentally be conscious of. The soles of your feet tell the story of where you have been and where you are going and should be considered when you are putting up your feet and kicking off your shoes at the end of a long day.

The energy center that extends out of the top of your head from your crown chakra is like an extended antenna. It is how you are pursuing the world around you. This is how you sense that it is about to rain, even when there isn't a storm cloud in sight yet, or how you get a feeling about the energy of a crowd when you walk into an office party. This chakra is your ability to receive input from the world around you from your eye level and up. It is less about the path you walk (foot chakras) and more about what other things are happening outside of you, for you to take in and respond to.

These 5 additional chakras comprise a more sensory impact on your whole chakra system. You are experiencing and pulling the world in around you and giving it to your main chakra system. All of this links to your perception, brain function, physical consciousness and more.

Your entire chakra system is the subtle, ethereal body of experience that strongly correlates with physical, mental and emotional path you take every day. Having knowledge about this energetic cycle will help you unfold and unravel more of what lies under your surface and how it can cause a lot of distortion, imbalance and challenge when not properly dealt with and nurtured.

Moving forward into the next chapter, you will take your new knowledge of the chakras and learn more about what kinds of issues can arise specific to each chakra. We will once again go through each layer, from the root to the crown, and explore the deficiencies, excesses, imbalances and blocks that can show up in your life and more about the process of what it means to heal your energy.

Chapter 4: The Health of the Chakras

The chakras play a vital role in the overall health of every person's body, mind and spirit. As you have learned in the previous chapter, each one has a specific correspondence to an emotional/mental energy and expression. The chakras are also closely linked to organ systems and glandular functions, helping the body to regulate the necessary performance required to live a healthy and whole life.

Not all of the symptoms that you experience in your life can be healed or controlled by your chakra energy and so if you are experiencing a medical condition, ask your doctor or healthcare provider for more information. As noted before, the chakras work in correlation to the entire bodily, mind and emotional framework and they must all be treated in specific ways in order to find the right solution for health and wholeness.

Since the book is not meant to replace medical advice from a doctor, use this knowledge to compliment any medical or health concerns that you may be experiencing.

Exploring your chakra health can be a long and challenging quest to know yourself on another level and therefore requires time, patience and compassion on your part, as you work to discover ways to allow for more energetic balance on your daily life. Looking at the chakras for help is an excellent way to understand the health of the chakras and why they make a difference on the health of your whole being.

To give you an idea of how this can manifest, let's look to each chakra for evidence. You will read through each chakra one by one to get an idea of how you might be feeling when your chakras are in a good balance, followed by a report of some of the physical and emotional blockages and imbalances that can come up for you in your physical and emotional well-being.

As you read, make special note of any areas that might jump out for you and your energy. There could be some relationships to your chakras causing some imbalances and usually, they are all working together in certain ways to compensate for other's imbalances and blockages.

There are plenty of ways to understand these imbalances and blockages and it first helps to know what you will feel like in each chakra and in your whole system when you are not blocked and are flowing freely.

The Chakras in Optimum Energy Flow

When you are in total support of your wholeness from your feet to the top of your head, you are in optimum energetic flow. This state of being is not easy to get to because it requires a lot of different elements to maintain, such as physical exercise or activities, dietary support, emotional support and healing of wounds and trauma, creative outlets, positive self-expression and so much more.

Part of the journey of healing your chakras involves the reality of making a lot of life changes to support a healthier you and live your life in a better balance with your whole being. You don't have to be an expert on any of these things and for every person the journey looks different as it is based on your unique and individual qualities. This book serves a general guide to help anyone understand the energetic quality of healthy chakras and what that balance can truly feel like. Within each chakra is the vibrational frequency where it feels the most balanced and clear. This section follows through each chakra to explain more of how it looks at optimum flow.

The Root Chakra

Qualities and Characteristics:

Survival, security, abundance, groundedness, primal energy, life-spark, ancestors and heritage, family issues, stability, Earth

An optimum energy flow in the root chakra will manifest in the following ways:

- Feelings of internal and external security and wealth

- Stability in all areas of life especially, home and financial experiences

- Calm and centered energy, firmly rooted to the Earth

- Healthy family dynamics and relationships

- All of your needs are being met

- Connection to your primal wisdom

- Rooted in yourself worth and ability to have what you need to thrive

- Flexibility in knees, legs and feet

- Healthy bowel movements

The Sacral Chakra

Qualities and Characteristics:

Creativity, joy, emotions, sensuality, passion, desire, one-on-one connections, intimacy, sexuality, fertility, Water

An optimum energy flow in the root chakra will manifest in the following ways:

- Positive connection to your emotional self

- Accepting of creative life force/ ability to live life creatively

- Open to your sensuality and passion

- Healthy sex drive and sexual partnerships

- Confidence with intimacy

- Feelings of joy and a desire to dance

- Emotional agility and groundedness

- Confident in close one-on-one connections

- Strong fertility and/or desire to procreate

- Healthy bladder function

- Regular menstruation

The Solar Plexus Chakra

<u>Qualities and Characteristics:</u>

Personal power, strength, energy, vitality, drive, ambition, action, life-force, self-confidence, identity, power, Fire

An optimum energy flow in the root chakra will manifest in the following ways:

- Connection to personal power and authority

- Strong ambition to accomplish daily tasks and goals, as well as life-long goals

- Strong sense of personal identity

- Energy to get up and go and set things in motion

- A regular desire to take action in all life matters

- Urge to do physical things, like sports, exercise, yoga, etc.

- Strength, both physical and mental, to carry forward with the task at hand

- Healthy digestive system function

- Healthy, regular metabolism

The Heart Chakra

Qualities and Characteristics:

Love, compassion, kindness, brotherly-love, unconditional love, friendship, partnership, collaboration, universal love, bonding, Air

An optimum energy flow in the root chakra will manifest in the following ways:

- Sense of compassion of all people, even strangers

- An ability to offer without expecting anything in return

- Capable of receiving love when it is offered

- Ability to love the self unconditionally

- Capacity of forgiveness; attitude of forgiveness

- Strongly bonded friendships and partnerships, even with colleagues

- Love for all creatures on the Earth, and for human beings in general

- Strong and healthy cardiovascular function

- Healthy blood pressure and circulation

- Healthy lymphatic flow

The Throat Chakra

<u>Qualities and Characteristics:</u>

Self-expression, communication with the self, communication with others, truthful expression, ability to listen, Sound

An optimum energy flow in the root chakra will manifest in the following ways:

- Capacity to express feelings, ideas, thoughts, and information well

- Honesty and truth in all matters

- Ability to listen well to others and hear their communication

- Positive ability to effectively communicate wants, desires and needs

- Ability to verbally stand up for oneself, beliefs, values, a cause, or a community

- Clear and direct verbal expression and communication

- Ability to physically hear well; healthy and open ears

- Clear and healthy lungs

- Healthy vocal cords and throat

The Brow Chakra

Qualities and Characteristics:

Intuition, wisdom, intellect, clairvoyance, inner sight, astral projection, creative visualization, psychic abilities, dreams, Light

An optimum energy flow in the root chakra will manifest in the following ways:

- Developed intuition, or intuitive sense

- Clear knowing and understanding through the intellect

- Focused and able to concentrate easily

- Strong capacity to visualize in the mind's eye, or third eye

- Acceptance of inner wisdom

- Healthy and strong cognitive abilities and memory

- Ability to recall dreams easily

- Possibilities of psychic awareness and clairvoyance

- Regular and restful sleep

The Crown Chakra

Qualities and Characteristics:

Collective consciousness, connection to divine source, expressions of gratitude, transcendence, enlightenment, oneness with All, Thought

An optimum energy flow in the root chakra will manifest in the following ways:

- Sense of belonging to the world and everyone and everything in it

- Spontaneous urges to do community service or help others in need, including strangers

- Feelings of wanting to work in large communities or groups that support a worthy cause

- A desire to make charitable donations

- Expansion of consciousness and a desire to seek answers to deeper questions

- Visual expressions of spiritual energies might be seen

- Thoughts are geared towards helping and healing the self and others

- Higher ideas and wisdom

- Healthy gland function and hormonal balance

- Awakened state; enlightened

All of these energetic realities are optimum flow possibilities when the chakras are balanced, clear and free to vibrate at normal levels. It is common to experience a lot of these realities even when you have discord in the chakras and its all about regaining this level of vibration with the self, throughout the experience and during your approach to healing and balancing your energy.

There are a variety of other ways that these energies can manifest and it is up to the individual to understand through your own unique journey to enlightenment, how these energies respond, react and relate to your personal growth story.

Now, there are several ways that the chakras are inclined to manifest imbalances, ailments and other issues and the next section will offer the offer point on the spectrum of how blockages, deficiencies and excesses can appear in your whole body and life.

Imbalances and Blockages: Emotional and Physical

The disturbances in your energy centers are akin to what it looks like when you have a cold, or indigestion and even crippling anxiety or excessive worry or doubt. All of these physical symptoms and emotional expressions are a part of the energy cycling through your body and can be seen as a sign that something is off kilter in the energy of your whole world within.

You can go to a doctor or a therapist to treat these symptoms and issues, however they are not likely to direct any information or support towards healing your energetic imbalances in your chakras and so you can take that energetic healing work into your own hands. There are professionals who do work with energy clearing and there are usually working as Reiki practitioners, acupuncturists, massage therapists, and body workers.

As each chakra has its own frequency, traits, and correspondences to physical, mental and emotional attributes, they all have their unique way of demonstrating that they are blocked or imbalanced. The following examples are some of the ways that you might experience these energetic misalignments, chakra by chakra.

The Root Chakra

Imbalances and Blockages:

- Excessive fear about minimal or minor issues

- Chronic fatigue

- Muscle and joint pain, especially in the hips, thighs, knees and feet

- Weak joints and muscles

- Hip dysplasia

- Sciatica

- Constipation

- Panic attacks about financial security or lack

- Feelings of homelessness (without being literally homeless)

- Aggressive or angry

- Easily frustrated

- Having a hard time settling down anywhere

- Deeply rooted family trauma, or karma

- Early childhood wounds, especially those that are blocked from memory

- Often feeling insecure about the self or your place in life

- Instability in work or career

- Unable to make ends meet

- Fearful of taking any risks or chances

- Low stamina

- Difficulty cultivating relationships because of low self-worth

- Greediness, both in wealth and with affection, or other ways of giving

- Being implacable

So much of the root chakra blocks and imbalances have to go with your feelings of security, safety and survival. If your survival or security has ever been threatened, even in early childhood development, your root chakra can easily hold onto that energy and it will therefore influence your life choices and the way that you act on certain realities in your life. Practicing an open root chakra can be hard if you have struggled with it your whole life, and finding the source of the block or imbalance can involve some deep digging into your past, allowing repressed childhood memories to surface. This can be hard to do alone and many people will choose to engage with a therapist in order to process some of these difficult emotions.

The pendulum always swings both ways and when there is an excess in the chakra, a person might be overly greedy and unwilling to share or part with anything they have struggled to attain or own. This also bleeds into other chakras, but the root of it is in the root, get it?

Pay attention to how you feel about your sense of security and your survival by asking yourself some of the following questions:

1. Do I feel like all of my needs are being met?

2. Do I struggle to attain what I want for my personal survival?

3. Am I at home with myself and my physical space?

4. Do I feel like I have two legs to stand on, literally and metaphorically?

5. Did I feel nurtured and provided for when I was young, or like I wasn't allowed to have what I needed and wanted?

These are excellent questions to begin asking yourself as you start to consider any potential blocks and imbalances in your root chakra.

The Sacral Chakra

Imbalances and Blockages:

- Lack of sex drive

- Excessive sex drive

- Difficulty processing emotions and over-expressing emotional sensitivities

- Blocked or stagnant creative flow

- Infertility

- Impotency

- Endometriosis

- Urinary tract infections

- Frigidity

- Fear of romantic partnerships and intimacy

- Chronic low back pain

- Lack of passion in anything you do

- Perception of being unlovable because of lack od desire or feelings of "coldness"

- Desire to do something creative and always finding an excuse not to do it

- Whimsical thinking that leads to an emotional let-down when the fantasy doesn't come true

The blockages and imbalances in the sacral chakra will have a lot to do with your sensual self. If you are blocked here you may have depression about your lack of sexual interaction, or even just a lack intimacy with your partner. It can feel like you are stuck, but also like you are undesirable. This goes hand in hand with your self-esteem which can show up in other chakras and often the root and solar plexus chakras are experiencing imbalance when your self-esteem and self-worth on the line.

In this case, it would be regarding your body, attractiveness to another sex, and relationship to your own sensual nature. You will also find here that if you are an artist or creative type, there will be stagnation in your ability to follow through with any projects, leaving you feeling stuck and not sure how to get out of the rut. Sometimes, too, for someone who has spent their whole life verifying that they are just not a creative person, might be suffering from a chronic imbalance in this area.

Another huge reality of this chakra is sexual trauma. Many people have possibly experienced sexual assault, rape, or other severe sexual traumas that will cause such and intense dam in the waters of the sacral chakra that it will take years to dislodge. This kind of block would require the attention and assistance of a trained therapist to help someone process their emotional and physical experience, in addition to doing the work with the energy healing, to help solve such a severe wound.

Pay attention to how you feel about your sensuality, sexuality and your creativity and emotional agility by asking yourself some of the following questions:

1. How do I feel about myself when someone wants to explore intimacy?

2. Am I uncomfortable when other people touch my body, or do I feel elated and energized?

3. How long do I linger on an emotion I am experiencing? Does it last for days or weeks, or just aa few hours or moments?

4. If I start a creative project, how likely am I to finish it?

5. After I have a sexual experience with someone, how do I feel? Revived and pleasureful, or uncomfortable and discontent?

There are a number of ways that you may be experiencing a blocked sacral chakra, so don't limit yourself to just these questions. Spend time reflecting on the quality of your intimacy, creativity and desire to learn more from your own experience.

The Solar Plexus Chakra

Imbalances and Blockages:

- Low energy

- Chronic fatigue syndrome

- Selfishness

- Aggressive self-confidence

- Overly competitive

- Defiant and disagreeable

- Fear of standing out in a crowd or being noticed

- Lack of drive or ambition to accomplish, or even set goals

- Digestive issues, such as indigestion, IBS, gastroenteritis

- Excessive weight gain around the middle

- Trouble metabolizing sugars

- Feeling uncertainty about what you like, what you want, or who you are

- Diminished self-esteem and lack of healthy ego

- Self-righteousness

- Passiveness

- Blaming other people for a lack of willpower or low self-worth

- Fighting with others over who is "right"

- Bossiness

- Difficulty getting up in the morning

- Lack of physical stamina

Since the solar plexus chakra is all about identity and personal power, you will have a variety of issues that can determine what type of imbalance or blockage you might have. In the instance of having a deficiency of energy in this chakra, you will have a low self-esteem, lack of drive, passivity, and problems effectively demonstrating your identity to the world around you. Conversely, an excess will manifest as a person who is aggressively self-righteous, demanding, bossy and overly critical of others who are not up to their standards. This excess can actually also be interpreted as a compensation for a greater lack of healthy solar plexus energy, making every effort to appear to have personal power when one does not.

The energy of this chakra is as important as all of the others and as a central point for energy has a way of determining the quality of energies in other parts of your system. Your whole identity is resting and residing here, and will therefore have a greater influence on the way that you project the other energies out into the world and through your own consciousness.

To find out what kind of block or imbalance you have in your solar plexus chakra, try asking yourself some of the following questions:

1. When someone at the office wants to present an idea on a project do I feel jealousy and anger, or sad and ashamed?

2. When I wake up in the morning do I feel determined to get going, or lackluster and lethargic?

3. When someone asks me what I do for a living do I feel embarrassed, or defensive?

4. When I am shown someone else's success story do I feel envious or do I feel angry?

5. Do I feel like I have a healthy self-confidence in all aspects of my life or do I feel either a) that I need to hide my true self, or b) make sure everyone knows how amazing I am at all times?

These sample questions are just to get you started with looking for the balance in your solar plexus chakra, and some of the answers to these questions might reflect that you have a healthy sense of self. Your personal power is an important part of you and involves some direct honesty about how you truly feel about yourself and not what other people might be thinking about you.

The Heart Chakra

<u>Imbalances and Blockages:</u>

- Disconnection from other people to avoid getting hurt emotionally

- Overly guarded and protective

- Unwilling to open up to people, even those who are offering you love and affection

- Discouragement from the inner self

- Longing for love without ever taking any chances on it

- Self-critical and judgmental

- Judgmental and critical of others

- Lack of compassion

- Being over giving and over sacrificing to the point of becoming a martyr

- Difficulty giving love as well as receiving love

- Absorbing other people's feelings and making them your own

- Circulation problems

- High blood pressure/ low blood pressure

- Cardiac issues, such as arteriosclerosis, heart murmur, etc.

- Indulging in sweets or other treats to "fill the void"; emotional eating

- Pain in the chest

- Feeling cautious around new people or new friends

- Fear of rejection

The heart wants to love so much. When we are children, the only thing we want is to be nurtured, reassured, held, have our physical needs met and be loved. Our earliest life experiences are where the first blocks and imbalances can really take hold of the energy in the heart chakra. Like with the root chakra, the heart holds onto a lot of things early on and can determine the way that you love others for the rest of your life, or until you learn some other lessons and allow your relationships to heal the wounds that may have been incurred in childhood.

Even as we get older, the wounds we sustain after a long and hard break up, or the loss of a loved one and the grief experienced as a result, will lead to some discordant energies that can be hard to balance out quickly. It can take time to heal the heart. Our experiences inform our energy, and when your heart has been hurt by an experience, you hold onto that energy and it will impact your future "heart-felt" experiences. Having a healthy heart chakra includes knowing how to heal yourself through your own personal compassion and self-love. It is important to connect the issues of the heart chakra not only to the way we explore love with others, but especially how we love ourselves.

To find out where you might be feeling some imbalance in your heart chakra, ask yourself some of these questions:

1. Am I always giving love to others but feeling like I never get anything in return?

2. Do I feel accepting of my flaws, faults, mistakes and personality at all times?

3. When I let go of a partnership, do I reject love and stay away from it, or hope for a more compatible experience moving forward?

4. Am I comfortable with being alone with myself, or do I need someone to be there with me all of the time?

5. Am I compassionate to the person in the parking lot who aggressively stole my parking spot?

These questions will help you start the ball rolling with asking the right questions for the heart chakra imbalances or blockages you may be experiencing. They will help you to get your mind in the thinking zone about what the heart wants and how it can respond to life situations that might be challenging to the heart.

The Throat Chakra

Imbalances and Blockages:

- Difficulty telling the truth

- Tendency to hold back in conversations, even when you have something valuable to contribute

- Fear of saying the "wrong" thing

- Purposefully over-talkative to avoid dealing with real feelings

- Overly expressive and unable to let anyone else speak because of an excessive need to talk about yourself

- Difficulty listening to others when they have something valuable to say

- Lying

- Sensitivity to being judged or criticized about how you speak or communicate your thoughts, ideas, or feelings

- Afraid to express your true feelings or self

- Frequent sore, or scratchy throat

- Ear trouble, like blocks, aches, tinnitus

- Chronic jaw pain and tightness

- Teeth grinding

- Feeling uncomfortable breaking open after a long period of silence

- Preference for total quiet and sensitivity to loud noises

- Talking over people

The energy of how you communicate is viscerally impactful since it is how all of your chakras talk to the outside world. It happens to be the only chakra that produces audible energy and as such, it makes sense that if you are feeling off, angry, upset, sad, or any other feeling, that you will make sound to describe and demonstrate what your energy and feelings sound like.

So, with that said, consider how a block or any other imbalance in your whole chakra system will manifest through your throat chakra. It is a valuable place to help you process your feelings, thoughts and ideas. "Talk therapy" has become more popular since the days of Freud and has allowed for people to find ways of analyzing and processing their emotions through the energy of sound and the expression through words of how they are feeling.

When you are unable to accurately express yourself, or connect your truth to your voice, you can have some difficulty clearly expressing your personality, your opinions and your true feelings and emotions. To get an idea of how your throat chakra might be blocked, start asking yourself questions like this:

1. When I am involved in a deep conversation with friends or acquaintances, am I confident in speaking my opinion, or do I stay quiet most of the time?

2. When I am talking to a stranger about who I am and what I do, do I feel like I am being totally honest about myself, or do I hold back information?

3. When I am with a friend and have a lot to say, do I feel like they get an equal opportunity to talk and express themselves, too?

4. After I have had a lot of quiet alone time, am I excited to get into a conversation, or do I want to stay quiet?

5. If I am called on in class, or work, to answer a question, do I get uncomfortable, shy, nervous, ashamed, or confused?

Use these sample questions to start asking more about how your throat chakra is feeling. Use the checklist above to ask yourself if you have any of the possible symptoms.

The Brow Chakra

<u>Imbalances and Blockages:</u>

- Insomnia

- Chronic headaches or migraines

- Bad dreams and nightmares

- Paranoia

- Problems with eyesight or other eye related illnesses and disorders

- Challenges making choices

- Mental illness

- Dementia

- Poor cognition, or inability to think clearly

- Hyper focused on details and unable to see the big picture

- Easily distracted; challenges with focus

- Sinus problems

- Forehead tension

- Panic attacks

- Thoughts of futility and a desire to give up

- Inability to look within and see an image with your eyes closed

Not all of these symptoms will occur and it can also depend on genetics and other life factors, so when you are assessing your own energy and blockages or imbalances, consider that there will be a lot of reasons for any specific issue. The third eye is in a place in your skull and will be related to a majority of mental health issues as well as the connection to the pineal gland and hormone secretion there. This gland is responsible for your circadian and other body rhythms, but was also considered by several ancient cultures to be the seat of your psychic power.

If you are blocked or imbalanced in this chakra, you may be having a hard time seeing past the end of your nose, let alone into the cosmic reality of the third eye. You can have a lot of difficulty expanding into a higher level of consciousness when you are blocked in this area and so it is worth the work to help yourself replenish an energetic balance in this area.

Often times, we lose a healthy vibration in this chakra when we are children, when we are told to grow up and stop pretending, or that our realities, dreams, and make-believe aren't real. It is a way to close off to your intuition and to lack trust in your ability to toot your own horn and trust your own inner wisdom.

Play around with different ideas of what you remember from being a kid and how it felt when you were off in your own world, practicing what you knew to be your reality. Explore the possible problems or issues in this chakra by considering some of the following:

1. Do you have issues with your ability to mentally focus on tasks, even when they are important to you, or something you are passionate about?

2. Is it hard for you to turn your thoughts off at the end of the day, especially while you are trying to fall asleep?

3. Do you puzzle over the same issues over and over again without ever finding a solution and answer?

4. Do you struggle with mental health issues, or a feeling like you don't fit in with how everyone else thinks and feels?

5. Do you get uncomfortable at night before bed because you are afraid of what dreams you might have?

Look at some of these possibilities and keep asking questions. Your third eye is how you connect to your true knowing on your path and the place that allows you to stay open to your higher mind. Blocks here create challenges for a person to become powerful with wisdom and intuition.

The Crown Chakra

Imbalances and Blockages:

- Disconnection from people in general; isolation

- Fear of other people or the whole world being against you

- Judgmental of other cultures, or having rigid beliefs about the way everyone should be

- Chronic headaches and/or migraines

- Spaciness, fogginess and lack of clarity

- Being mentally distant when around other people

- Mental health issues

- Depression and/or anxiety

- Existential crises

- Nervous breakdown

- Feeling lost and not knowing where to turn

- Problems with society and culture and feeling connected to it/ or disconnected from it

- General feelings of incompatibility with social groups

- Tension in the upper neck, jaw and shoulders

- Denial about your true self and true nature

- Disconnection from what matters most to you

- Overly rational and intellectual attitude towards all life circumstances

- Shameful feelings about not doing enough for your family, or cultural group

- Disconnect between the self and others beliefs about you

The crown chakra is how we connect to everything outside of ourselves as ourselves. It is the place that allows us to experience enlightenment, however if we are resistant to becoming enlightened, then we will have major struggles, blocks and issues arise in our lives that can lead to some of the above-mentioned symptoms. Not all of these issues will arise, and again, it depends on your unique experience.

The crown is also about your wholeness and your honesty in all of your other chakras. If you are struggling to achieve enlightenment and fully embrace opening in the crown, it could be because you need to revisit other areas in your energy for more haling and transformation. This practice will help you engage with what parts of you need the most healing, most frequently, and the crown is a good example of how to help yourself identify the blocks in other areas.

For example, if you are feeling incompatible with social groups, tendencies to isolate, and fear of other people and what they will do to you, then you might be dealing with a root chakra block that made you feel like you can trust anyone, because you learned in childhood from your caregivers that it isn't safe to trust the people around you, or that you cannot be yourself freely around others safely. That feeling of not feeling safe to be yourself can direct you to your solar plexus where you see the blocks of personal identity show up.

This method of understanding your whole system can take time and practice, however, when dealing with the crown, you can begin to understand the links between the issues in your chakras and will have a better way of understanding how to heal those imbalances.

Because the crown chakra is closely linked to transcendence and enlightenment, it can take a long time to work through this area and really open it up. People spend their whole lives looking for those answers and reaching those levels of awakening and it is certainly worth the effort. You may have to do some significant work in other, lower chakras before you can fully engage with the power of your crown. Some possible questions to ask when dealing with crown chakra imbalances are:

1. Do I feel connected to the whole Universe and see that we are all connected to each other by dynamic forces?

2. Do I live in fear and feelings that everyone is against me, or will be against me at some point?

3. Are there times when I struggle to see the answers to life's deeper questions?

4. Do I spend anytime actually asking deeper questions about life, the self and why we are all here?

5. Do I work on myself so that I can understand my place in this world better, or do I expect the world to work for me?

The crown chakra takes you on a deeper and much bigger quest, beyond just the self and into the arms of the whole Universe and its energy. It can be a challenging and frightening time, hence why many people will stay away from enlightenment and will focus on other life matters, staying at the surface of reality and never looking further.

Practice asking some of these questions and others to get you familiar with your crown chakra.

Healing the Chakras

With all of your new knowledge about how the chakras work and how they become imbalanced, you can begin to feel excited about working towards making healing shift and transforming your frequency to resonate at a higher vibration. This effort is what led you to this book in the first place and why you will get a better knowing of yourself and the world around you, as you practice the work of healing your chakras.

Healing the chakras is not something you can do in a long weekend, or even over the course of a several months. For a lot of people, it can take years of practice and unravelling, rebuilding the mind and the body to understand the whole system of energy that you have always lived with, but were never shown how to heal or help.

The best advice for healing the chakras is to take it slow and don't try to rush the experience. It can be an ongoing process and it will become a part of your daily or weekly health care routine with the right approach and consistent attention.

When you are working with your own energy, a lot of dormant energies will rise to the surface and this can include uncomfortable memories, traumatic experiences, painful moments, and many emotions, thoughts and ideas that will be challenging to work through and identify.

It is a part of the journey to knowing the self to do this work and it is something we can all give to ourselves when we are ready. You may get started and feel a lot of impactful changes and although it feels like it is going well, all of a sudden out of nowhere, you will have a week long bout of depression and fatigue. This is not a bad thing and will often indicate that you are making some progress.

When these types of things occur, it can mean that your energy is working to rid itself of a past pain, issue, or belief that you had, and you are feeling it on the physical and emotional level by having to endure this week of sorrow. The support you give to yourself at these times is what will really help you evolve and rebalance more quickly and that is a great way to help yourself heal on a forward track.

Sometimes, we will revert back to damaging and unhealthy patterns when things come up and resurface, or emotions get too deep and dark. It can be hard to fully rebalance your chakras when you are unable to make a significant change and are relying on your patterns and behaviors to keep you "safe" in the identity you have always known.

This is why it becomes so challenging for people to ignite this process: it leads you down the road of purging and cleansing all of the negative thoughts, ideas, patterns, memories, and various other issues from your energetic system and that gives people a lot of uncomfortable results.

If you can offer yourself an attitude of compassion and understanding during your "purging" moments, then you will more quickly heal the blocks in your system. An example of this might be taking long walks to reflect and contemplate in nature, eating balanced, home-cooked meals, having a long bath and tucking yourself in early, as opposed to, staying in bed in the dark all day, avoiding the outside world, drinking or using substances for comfort and binging unhealthy foods to fill the void.

As you get more involved with looking to your chakras for answers about your health, energy and purpose, you will gain a better feel for how to aid yourself in the more challenging moments. You can be very helpful to your healing process when you use your intuition, instinct and good judgement. Here is a list of some of the beneficial ways you can support healing your chakras:

- Spend time in nature and connect with the world around you in a meaningful way.

- Let go of addictions, be they sweets, snacks, drugs, alcohol, or other.

- Focus on an empathic and kind approach, instead of critical or demeaning, when talking to yourself during your journey.

- Eliminate possible triggers ahead of time.

- Tend to all levels of yourself by having a regular check-in, asking "How is my body feeling? My mind? My heart? My spirit?"

- Feast on healthy and nutritious foods and drink plenty of water.

- Move your body around, even if you are lying on the floor and just kicking your legs in the air, or swinging your arms around yourself.

- Visit places that are inspiring to you.

- Talk to someone you trust about your experiences.

- Start a journal or a diary to reveal your experience to yourself so you can get your thought and feeling energy out onto paper.

- Give yourself plenty of rest, including ample sleep at night.

- Create boundaries with people, places, or things that hinder your progress, or take you back to your old patterns and behaviors that you are trying to change.

- Use your voice to talk about your experience.

This list is just a general outline of some of the ways that you can really help influence a healthier chakra healing and rebalancing journey. You can learn all kinds of different ways to support yourself that feel aligned with who you are as a person so that you can truly embrace the quality of life you are looking for.

There are plenty of ways that you can get off track from your healing experience and if you keep looking ahead at where you want to be, you will find your destination in no time.

Give yourself time and patience, compassion and love as you begin this exciting journey and look for ways to give yourself support along the way. The next chapter will provide you with ways that you can promote healing and rebalancing in your chakras. All of the methods in the next chapter are proven tools to help you align your chakras to their highest vibration.

Chapter 5: Methods for Chakra Healing

Who you are and how you live your life is entirely unique and we all have the right to decide how we want to go on a healing quest to help ourselves transform. When you are working with your chakras you will have an experience that no one else will have because no one else has lived your life, or is exactly like you. So, when you are going through this chapter of methods for chakra healing, keep all of these facts in mind.

Part of healing is listening to your intuition and allowing it to help you move forward. If something doesn't feel right, right now, you can wait a little longer to practice something or use a specific healing technique until your body feels flexible enough for it, or you have more energy or opening to receive the lessons that are coming up for you to resolve.

The power of healing the chakras and becoming acquainted with how they function and inform your daily existence, is such an enlivening and enlightening quest that will take a lot of connection to yourself and your experiences, both from the past and the present, as you look towards filling in the role of the future self you are working to become.

The methods that you will learn about in this chapter have been used for centuries in various ways in order to alter your vibrational frequency and attain new levels of self-awareness and enlightenment. After all, the point of healing your chakras is to transcend the human drama and live in a freer, healthier way, and so the work that you do to get there will be all about how you involve yourself in your journey.

The more often you concentrate on healing these parts of yourself, the more quickly you will arrive at your desired outcomes, and keep in mind that your desired outcome is likely to shift and change throughout the process as you work harder to dig more deeply into the caves of your human consciousness.

This journey is deep and goes way beneath the surface of what you are projecting into your life as you know it. It will bring to attention all of the hidden reasons for how you have been behaving, why you have held yourself back in certain ways, or how you have had imbalances in your body or mind for so long.

The methods you will learn here are only the beginning and are very simple tools for any beginner to get started with awakening and rejuvenating the chakras. The plan you create for yourself as you use this information is entirely up to you and you can find out even more about these subjects and others related to mind-body-spirit connection, in order to have a fuller growth journey.

There will be several sections to pour over including ways that will help you find the right resources or environments to do this energy work in. You may also decide at a certain point to join a class or a community involved in these practices to push you forward even more as you heal.

Enjoy bringing these methods and practices to life in your regular self-care routines and witness yourself open more and more through the expansion and healing process. You may want to keep a journal regularly to keep notes on your progress. It can be very beneficial to look back on where you started or when you were working on certain chakras to see proof and evidence of how much you have grown and changed over time.

Some of these methods might require that you obtain tools from a shop, or go to a location outside of your home, but overall they will be simple, affordable and accessible for everyone to enjoy. All you need is yourself and the readiness to begin your healing journey!

Crystal Healing

Crystals are considered "in-organic" by the scientific community. That may be true, but if you have ever held one in your hand, you may have noticed or sensed the energy emitting from the stone, and how alive it feels. Crystals and gemstones are formed inside of the Earth through intense pressure, water and other chemical compounds that help to "grow" these unique elements.

You have seen many ladies wearing diamond engagement rings, no doubt. All of these were formed under very intense pressure and conditions to form one of the most expensive gems around. They are cut in specific ways and set into rings in order to be worn by a bride to be, or someone who is displaying their love of something sparkling. Few people realize how powerful the energy emitted from a diamond actually is. It has a huge potential force of energy radiating off it, specifically because of how it was formed in the ground that it was mined from.

When you wear a diamond ring on your finger, or any other crystal or gemstone, your entire energy field is connecting to that same energy and aligning with that frequency. It can be so subtle that no one would really notice it, especially if it is a small jewel, but when you are dealing with the larger rocks and crystals, you can feel a more potent and powerful energy pushing out of it.

Since you have learned about the science of chakras and the frequency that they radiate, then you can understand why and how crystals, which do the same thing, would have the same effect. Like you, a crystal will absorb and contain energy inside of it and so when people use healing stones and crystals for their work, you will often find that they will use energy clearing methods on their own crystals!

Harmonic resonance is something that can occur between two energies that will synchronize their energy flow in order to be in harmony with one another. Think of a rock band that plays songs together: they play notes that harmonize together and are sticking to a particular rhythm or beat, in order to make a song. All of the musicians synchronize their energy in order to play a song from beginning to end. If they didn't have harmonic resonance, the song would be all over the place and wouldn't sound very musical at all.

With crystals, you can achieve harmonic resonance between your energy and the energy of the crystal in order to regain or rebalance your own frequencies. You can enjoy a new kind of inner rhythm when you bring a crystal or gemstone close to your heart chakra, worn as a necklace, or to your root chakra when carried in your pocket.

For several people who are interested in using crystals for chakra healing therapy, you can simply add it to your meditations and yoga practices by physically laying the stone on top of each chakra placement on the body while you lie on your back.

Lying in position for several minutes with a large piece of quartz crystal, or kyanite on your abdomen, will effectively shift and recharge the energy of your solar plexus so that you can begin to go through a greater purging and processing of the emotions or blocks stored there.

To be clear, crystals don't magically eliminate the issues you are holding onto. The way that they work is to magnify the energy that you are holding onto that needs to be released, bringing it to the surface so that you can let go of it fully.

Let's see an example of that: Let's say after about 30 minutes of meditation with a crystal placed on your heart chakra, you get up feeling refreshed, relaxed, calm and excited to feel an open heart and new lease on love and life. Later that night, you start to feel really sad and depressed and will even burst into tears out of nowhere. You are having thoughts about your last relationship pop up, even though you feel completely over that experience and have nothing further to do with it. You are even happy for your ex, that they got married and found the right partner for themselves. So why are you thinking about your relationship and while feeling sad out of nowhere?

The answer is that as soon as you stopped using the crystal therapy in your afternoon meditation, your whole energy system began to shift and re-coordinate and after several hours of feeling like everything was going to work out just fine, you suddenly felt tragically sad. Your heart chakra was showing you exactly what was still blocking your ability to open up to a new lover, or partner. Even though you thought you were over it, you still had a residual energetic feeling of sorrow.

After recognizing this, let's say you do some journaling about that time in your life and you get to the part where your ex is happy and in love and a newly wed while you are still struggling to find the right partnership for yourself. You discover that you have feelings of happiness for your ex, however you are feeling a longing for what they have and a sense of not knowing if it will ever happen for you the way it happened for them.

All of this because you put a crystal on your heart chakra and meditated. Here's the thing though: if you are going to use crystals for chakra healing, don't expect a profound healing discovery every time you use one. It doesn't always work that way and it can take a lot of time and practice to effectively read the signals of your energy in order to interpret what is slapping you in the face to be healed and released.

Don't get discouraged if you don't have any big epiphanies or breakthroughs right off the bat. You can have a lot of other very profound, healing experiences when you work with crystals and they do have a powerful energetic impact on your whole energy system when regularly used, or even only used sporadically.

Because ever type of crystal has its own energy frequency, there are some that are more effective for certain chakras than others and the following list will be helpful for you, if you are not familiar with crystals and gemstones, to locate the right one for your healing needs:

- Root chakra: Black Tourmaline, Bloodstone, Carnelian, Garnet, Hematite, Tiger's Eye, Fiery Agate, Red Jasper, Smoky Quartz, Black Kyanite, Obsidian

- Sacral Chakra: Amber, Aragonite, Citrine, Carnelian, Orange Coral, Moonstone, Orange Aventurine, Orange Calcite, Red Jasper, Snowflake Obsidian,

- Solar Plexus: Citrine, Calcite, Yellow Tourmaline, Lemon Quartz, Sunstone, Peridot, Topaz, Malachite, Quartz Crystal, Amber, Yellow Jasper

- Heart Chakra: Green Calcite, Emerald, Jade, Rose Quartz, Rhodochrosite, Rhodonite, Green Tourmaline, Green Aventurine, Amazonite

- Throat Chakra: Turquoise, Angelite, Aquamarine, Celestite Crystal, Lapis Lazuli, Blue Calcite, Blue Amazonite, Blue Apatite, Scolecite,

- Brow Chakra: Quartz Crystal, Purple Fluorite, Labradorite, Shungite, Amethyst, Azurite, Black Obsidian, Sodalite

- <u>Crown Chakra</u>: Quartz Crystal, Diamond, Kyanite, Lepidolite, Selenite, Sugilite, Amethyst, Charoite, White Calcite

All of these stones are intended for each chakra to create a harmonic resonance that will leave you feeling awakened and aware, as well as to help you kick start some purging and cleansing of your chakra energy blockages. There are so many stones that are not on this list that will also be helpful in your healing experience. The best way to choose a stone for yourself is to hold it in your hand and see how well you resonate with that energy.

Some people feel that certain crystals and gemstones will "call" to them and have exactly the right energy that they need right then. Since your energy is never constant and always shifting and rebalancing, the kind of stone that you need will change from time to time as well. It can be useful to have a few to choose from and having a selection for healing purposes is a great goal to have.

There is another stone that is often used as a Universal chakra healing stone that has an ability to stay fully charged at its own frequency without needing to be cleansed of absorbed energy: Blue Kyanite.

This stone, since it does not collect negative vibrations, is a cleansing tool for other stones and crystals, as well as for your own chakra energy. In fact, it is known as the chakra healing stone as it has the power to help you align all of your chakras. This can be a great choice for a beginner to use since it will work well for every chakra as well as for the whole system of energy.

Using Blue Kyanite regularly during healing meditations and crystal healing work will show you how to effectively shift and alter your energy with one, simple piece of the Earth's treasures.

So, how do you heal yourself with crystals? As mentioned, you can simply lay them over each chakra as you meditate and there are a few other ways that you can use them to keep yourself in balance and focused on your healing:

- Wear them as jewelry everywhere you go, or carry them in your pocket.

- Add them to your bath water when you have a relaxing soak in the tub.

- Place them under your pillow to enjoy restful, healing sleep.

- Add them to your drinking water and let them infuse the water with healing vibration for you to drink.

- Put them in your shoes overnight so your feet will feel empowered while you walk around all day long.

- Rest them on the skin of your face to give you a youthful glow and vibrant skin.

- Plant them in the vegetable garden in your yard to infuse the soil and the food growing in it with high vibrational energy.

- Place them in a circle around your yoga mat so that they are beaming high vibrations to you while you work on your flexibility and strength.

These are just a few possibilities and you are likely to stumble across a few more in your daily life. The applications are endless! You will also need to keep your stones energetically "pure" for regular use. If they are absorbing negative energies and vibrations, then you will need to make sure that they are properly cleansed after using them a few times during healing meditations.

Here are some basic ways to keep your crystals and gemstones cleansed and free of unwanted vibrational energies:

- Place them in warm salt water for half an hour.

- Set them outside in the sun for several hours.

- Place them next to, or on top of, a piece of Blue Kyanite.

- Smudge them with incense (ancient purifying technique using smoke).

Try some of these methods to keep your crystals fresh and clean, ready for healing use.

In order to get the best benefit from healing with crystals, here is a general meditation that you can use on any chakra with a corresponding crystal or gemstone:

General Guidelines for Chakra Healing with Crystals:

1. Lie in a comfortable position on the floor, or on a bed or other surface.

2. Place the stone on the desired chakra.

3. Take several deep, relaxing breaths and connect to your body.

4. Through your breathing, connect to the energy of the stone. Concentrate on feeling its energy.

5. Allow yourself feel your own energy connecting to the stone. Pay close attention and continue breathing deeply and slowly.

6. Focus on your feelings in this area. What ideas/thoughts/images/memories are coming up for you here?

7. Spend time "listening" to your energy and allow it to surface as needed. Experience the energy of its manifestation and let it flow into the stone resting on your chakra.

8. Picture the negative ideas/thoughts/memories/images being released into the stone and leaving your body.

9. Visualize your chakra being recharged and bright in light. Feel the energy of this stone taking hold of your wounds and pain and relieving you of them.

10. Remove the stone from your chakra and meditate on how your energy feels. Allow yourself to process any

deeper feelings and emotions that might have surfaced. Be prepared for thoughts and feelings to surface later on, after you are done meditating.

These basic instructions are all you need to get you started with healing with crystals. You can apply these basic steps to every chakra and it will take as little as 10 minutes to as long as an hour. You are going to find a lot of healing energy from these little Earth treasures, and the more you use them, the better you will heal. They can be quite impressive in their abilities and will really help you magnify the issues that need unblocking. Consider using them in every chakra meditation you do to get you started on your healing path.

Moving forward into the next section, you will learn what Yoga is and how it has an impact on your chakra energy.

Yoga Practices

By this point you have probably heard of yoga, at least a few times, and have seen it or practiced it on your own. You may also know people, friends and colleagues who talk about their yoga practice that they go to twice a week and how great it has been for their health and vitality.

As you learned in *Chapter 1: History of Chakras*, the concept and theory behind your swirling vortices of energy came from the ancient Sanskrit texts known as the Vedas in the Hindu religion. These texts were the source of many religious, spiritual and cultural practice and are continuing to be practiced today.

These practices have also made their debuts in other countries and cultures and today, Yoga is one of the most practiced forms of physical fitness and wellness-care in Western culture, as well as where it originated from. It has become a regular institution of the modern world and has been known for centuries for its healing benefits and ability to increase life span, encourage healthy muscles, bones and tissues, and help the practitioner enter a transcendent state of calm through the use of postures, breathing techniques, and meditation.

The world of yoga is vast and there are a variety of practices, beliefs and techniques that have been developed by various gurus, bringing more knowledge and identity to each type of yoga and the purpose of those practices. There are dozens of different styles of yoga, and here are the yoga practices that are most commonly practiced in the West today:

- **Hatha Yoga**- This is a broad term to incorporate a lot of different postures and poses that are often used in a variety of other yoga practices. The purpose of this style is to bring about more strength and physical vitality through better breath and posture. All of the poses are strength-building, or tend to be, and will be complimented by soothing stretch.

- **Ashtanga Yoga**- This style of yoga is much more physically demanding and is useful for a more advanced practitioner. The word Ashtanga translates to mean "eight-limb path" and is a very vigorous compliment to some of the more gentle and rebalancing yoga styles.

- **Vinyasa Yoga**- This, like Ashtanga, is a more advanced, quicker-paced and athletic form of yoga. It builds of the rigorous work of Ashtanga and makes for an even more challenging body work out. The outcome is to create greater flexibility, more powerful breath and deeper alignment with the whole being. The word Vinyasa translates to mean "to place in a special way."

- **Iyengar Yoga**- These poses are precise, slow, and involve a lot of breath control. This practice is meant to aid in alignment. There are very small adjustments made and usually props, like bolsters or stretching bands, will be utilized to perfect form and posture. It is a much more calming and deeply relaxing workout.

- **Bikram Yoga**- This style of yoga has become a sensation because it uses heat to help your body release toxins and work in a warmer room setting for optimum purging and cleansing. It would be like doing yoga in a sauna, usually at around 105 degrees F.

- **<u>Yin Yoga</u>**- Yin is the word to describe the divine feminine energy in each of us. Like the Iyengar practice, it is slow and relaxing and tends to be seated a majority of the time. In this practice, poses are held for much longer periods of time to allow for a deeper stretch. It is meant for healing, inner peace and relaxation.

- **<u>Jivamukti Yoga</u>**- Based on the Vinyasa practice, this style incorporates a great deal more chanting and spiritual teaching and guidance. It has more to do with being one with the Earth and everyone in it. You could say it is the exercise for opening the crown chakra.

- **<u>Kundalini Yoga</u>**- This style of yoga is best known for awakening the Kundalini energy at the base of the spine that will lead to a full chakra rebalancing and awakening journey to enlightenment. It is often called "the yoga of awareness". You might say that this is the yoga for the chakras to heal, however they are all capable of keeping your energy centers cleansed and clear. Kundalini is based on the dormant energy being sparked to life and so all of the poses are intended to wake your "snake" and bring all of your chakras into alignment.

All of these yoga styles can be a beneficial to your chakra healing work. As you read through them and got a sense of what they might be best for, as far as physical health is concerned, you may also have gotten an idea of which chakra they can be easily correlated with. Even though they will have a general purging and rebalancing effect, while working on a specific chakra, you might be more inclined to go for a certain style.

For example, if you are trying to invigorate your energy and heal the blocks in your solar plexus, your right to act and your personal power, then you might want to go for the Ashtanga or the Vinyasa style. If you are trying to be more open in your heart chakra, the Yin yoga poses and rhythm might be a better choice, while the Jivamukti style can be beneficial to exercising your openness to the Universal light in everyone and in all places on Earth.

Even if you are interested in doing only yoga poses that are in alignment with a specific chakra energy, you can build upon your overall physical, emotional, spiritual, and energetic strength by practices any one of these yoga styles.

For some, the idea of going to the Kundalini practice makes the most sense when working on healing the chakras. The term Kundalini refers to the "coiled-up" energy at the base of your spine, where your root chakra sits, and the idea behind this yoga is that you will practice opening that dormant life-force energy to heal the whole chakra system. It can take many years of practice to go through it like this and it is worth it in addition to a couple of other practices that will help you enhance your journey so that you can get there a little faster.

The best way to decide what style of yoga works for you and your chakra healing practices is to try a few different styles and see what makes you feel the most aligned and one with yourself. You can view some samples of these styles on line through instructional videos, or you can try some classes at the local yoga studio. There are yoga teachers and yoga studios in every city and town these days, and so it won't be hard to find this healing practice.

Even if you are feeling stuck in your chakra awakening and rebalancing, yoga can help you to reorganize your energy and get back on track, so that you feel better equipped and supported to continue your healing journey.

Meditations and Mindfulness

Many people today are being prescribed meditation in order to regain balance, practice inner peace, and heal the mind, body and spirit. This idea has come from a long line of practices, all coming from ancient times and across continents and cultures. Almost every religion has some form of what we call meditation and the point of it is to reconnect you to yourself, help you ground, and come into a place of inner knowing.

Meditation is often seen as part of a yoga practice, as well as being a separate experience that will help you reorganize the energy of how you are thinking, feeling, and expressing yourself. You can find so many different styles of meditation, and a lot of people will just take the simple idea of it and create their own unique style of meditation.

The general rule of thumb with any meditation practice is that you are able to sit quietly in an undisturbed way so that you can be in a reflective mind state to release any challenging thoughts or feelings. For some people, concentrating for several minutes at a time can be very difficult. We live in an incredibly stimulating world and our attention spans become more diminished as we find new and exciting ways to look at the world and participate in technology, information and entertainment.

To separate yourself from all of that outside chatter so that you can focus more deeply on your inside chatter, is part of the point of meditation and mindfulness. When you give space to your own inner world and you align with the power of your own energy, you make room for understanding what lies below your surface so that you can process it and heal it naturally.

Meditation brings all of your internal ideas, thoughts, and repressed wants and desires, as well as fears and insecurities, to the surface. When we are living in our daily lives, going to work, talking to colleagues, stuck in traffic, learning new things, socializing, scrolling through social media, binge-watching Netflix shows, taking care of our families and partners, we are focused on everything around us and outside of ourselves. This is true for anyone and there are hardly enough moments in a day to stop and reflect on your own inner world while you are working so hard to be present in your regularly scheduled routine.

Mindfulness is a form of meditation that creates a meditative state in whatever moment you are living in. That said, you would be living in your normal everyday life in a meditation, essentially. An example of that would be participating in a work meeting at the office. Normally, you might feel like you can't wait to get it over with, or uncomfortable because you didn't finish your report on time.

With mindfulness you would take those feelings to really understand the whole room around you, not just your own fears and concerns. You might look at every person around you and notice how they are feeling. You might carefully examine every pen and notebook on the conference table, noticing every detail. You could mindfully listen to every word every person is saying, so that you are clearly receiving all of the input form the entire experience, not just what you are feeling under the surface.

In a way, mindfulness meditation brings an opposite effect to a more classic form of meditation. Any regular meditation practice will ask you to go within to achieve calm and inner peace. Mindfulness shows you how to regard the world around you in a meditative state of mind, to incorporate the balance you would achieve if you were sitting with your eyes closed in a moment of quiet reflection.

So, what does all of this have to do with the chakras? Meditation and mindfulness are extremely nourishing to your whole energy system. When you practice meditation, you immediately begin to recalibrate, re-center and refresh your energy centers. The chakras are incredibly sensitive and receptive to this, because you have learned throughout this book, your energy centers work together with your body and your mind to achieve a state of wholeness.

Meditation is proven to give you a sense of calm, a lowered heart rate, a state of inner peace, and a whole-body relaxation. Achieving this kind of state on a regular basis will afford you the opportunity to transform, not only on the energetic level, but on the cellular level as well.

Studies show that people who meditate tend to live longer lives, have a general sense of peace and tranquility, tend to suffer illness less frequently then those who don't meditate, sleep better, and have a deeper connection to their internal energy as well as their external experiences.

You really don't have to study meditation to do it, or be good at it. All you need is presence to do it and a space to do it in. You can do it your car, in a park, on an airplane, in the office; there are no limits to how you can incorporate meditation into your life and as you get better at practicing it regularly, the easier it becomes to do it anywhere, anytime.

The following guidelines will offer you a simple and general meditation and mindfulness practice that you can engage with every day, or as often as you would like to:

General Guidelines for Meditation and Mindfulness

1. Find a space that feels most comfortable for you. Try to find an area where you won't be interrupted or disturbed.

2. In general, meditation is most comfortable in a seated position, or lying down. You can do it standing if you are wanting to approach it in that way. However you are most comfortable is the position you should start in. Try a seated position to begin.

3. Close your eyes and take some deep breaths in and out. Enjoy taking slow, deep breaths for several moments and center and ground yourself.

4. As you relax, notice any thoughts that might come into your head. Do not ignore what they are, or try to silence them. Note what the thoughts are, acknowledge them and continue with your meditative state.

5. You may want to notice if you can attribute any thoughts to a particular chakra, but in general, try to just focus on your energy and breath.

6. Your thoughts may stream through your mind for a while as you shift gears and recalibrate your energy to be in a state of calm and inner peace. Allow the thoughts to wash over you and then ebb away like the tide of an ocean.

7. Stay in this position until you feel total stillness of thought. (This may take practice, but don't give up. We can all get to this point in our consciousness).

8. When you get to the stillness in your mind, continue to relax and breath and release anything that you might still be holding onto.

9. Enjoy several minutes of just listening to your breath, your empty thoughts and the world around you.

10. When you are ready, open your eyes and begin to notice every little detail of the space you are in. Notice the scent, the temperature of the air and its stillness, or motion. Take note of the energy of the space and any

sounds. Notice the walls, or if you are in nature, the trees. Pay close attention to the details and get close to every moment.

11. Enjoy this state of mindfulness as long as you like, seeing, feeling and sensing the world around where you are sitting. This can help you bring your meditative mindset into the world outside of you so that you can achieve meditation in every moment you are existing in.

12. To reconnect to your daily life, close your eyes again and take a few deep breaths in and exhales out. Reach your hands above your head and press your palms together.

13. Pull your arms down so that you bring your hands in front of your heart, like they are praying. Take one last deep breath and go forward with your day.

This very simple meditation/mindfulness practice can be applied in a variety of ways to any chakra meditation you are doing. The essential purpose of a meditative state is to rearrange your energy to match the vibrational frequency of peace and inner calm so that all of your systems can function optimally.

Your thoughts are important, so even if you have mind chatter while you are engaging in this activity, it could be a good thing to help inform you of what is coming to the surface the most for resolution and attention. When you engage in meditation for the purpose of chakra healing and unblocking, your thoughts will be helpful in guiding you toward what needs to be healed and unblocked, or balanced.

In the next section, we will look at ways that you can incorporate a chakra healing technique to your already existing meditation and mindfulness practice by using creative visualization.

Chakra Visualization

In the beginning of this book, you used creative visualization to picture each of your chakras and become acquainted with where they are located and what color represents each one. You also learned that the third eye, or brow chakra (6th chakra) is where you are able to picture images inside of your mind. Creative visualization comes from this part of the mind and "sight" of the energy center in your forehead and can be very helpful on your healing journey to help you see what cannot be seen by the physical eyes.

As you structure your chakra healing process, you can incorporate the use of crystals and gemstones, yoga, meditation and mindfulness, and creative visualization. Picturing the action you want to achieve and the desired results has been proven to help people work through various mental, emotional, and physical issues. It is a great way for you to get in contact with the imagery of the self and to sense what is happening on an energetic level inside of your body.

A helpful way to understand creative visualization is to think about what it looks like when you are dreaming. When you are asleep at night, your unconscious mind is hard at work, interpreting the feelings, actions and energies of the day or the week through a series of images projected by your mind and internal brain waves. When you wake up, you try to remember what you "saw" in your dream while you slept and you are able to piece together a short film of that dreamworld experience.

Creative visualization is a lot like that, except you are awake and focused on what you are attempting to see, having more control over the images that are being projected in your mind. When you use this technique, coupled with your meditation and other tools and methods, you will achieve an even greater release and balance within your energy centers.

Any of your chakras can be meditated on one at a time during a healing ritual or practice, and you can also picture your whole chakra system while you work. The point is that you "see" the energy of these points in your body and connect to them one by one and as a whole.

The following creative visualization exercise, combined with a meditation, will give you an overview of how to work with the chakras one by one. In this case, you will be able to input whichever chakra you are needing to spend time looking at. You can modify these techniques as much as you want, as well. It is a creative process and can be unique to you and your style of imagination, creativity and healing.

General Guidelines for Creative Visualization and Chakra Healing

1. Begin your visualization practice by following the *General Guidelines for Mediation and Mindfulness.* You will want to be seated or lying down in a comfortable position and connecting to your breath to ground and center yourself.

2. Meditate for several moments with your breath, to relax your mind and prepare to work in your inner eye.

3. Start to picture the chakra center you are working on. Bring it into focus in your mind. See the center of it and how wide it is. See the color and its brightness or dullness. See the area of your body where it is located.

4. Spend time focusing on this energy and let yourself physically feel any energy in your system connected to this chakra center. What do you see when you look at this part of your body?

5. Allow any images or thoughts and ideas to pop up and acknowledge them. Communicate with them in your eye and mind and ask them what they need. If you are feeling tightness in this area, or stagnation, what is it

represented by? An image? An object? A memory? Use your creative visualization to truly see what the energy is holding onto here.

6. Play around with this area for a long time. Only try to see this one part of your body and don't yet focus on any other parts, unless you are being drawn to, or guided to other chakras by your intuition. Trust your inner guidance to support your healing visualization journey.

7. Let yourself stay with the images and ideas of this area you are working on. What happens to the energy when you try to change it through creative visualization? Practice altering the ideas, images, or thoughts into new pictures. (Ex: your heart ache looks like a really big elephant standing on top of your chest, so you shrink it down to a little mouse with sweet, beady little eyes that wants to nuzzle close to you for comfort and is much lighter and gentler and more tender)

8. Try to explore different ways of picturing and visualizing these transformations. Another example could be seeing a painful memory from childhood when your parents were fighting. You can transform the

memory to see your present self appearing in the memory and tenderly hugging your young self, offering energetic comfort to the experience through the visualization.

9. There are a lot of ways these energetic images or feelings can appear and you can decide the creative transformation you want to invoke. You can see it almost like lucid dreaming, having control over your dream state and making choices within that space to effectively alter the energy of the moment you are in.

10. Practice this visualization meditation for your chakra for as long as you need to.

11. Bring yourself back into focus by connecting to your physical body again. Bring your attention to your breath and see your whole body in your mind's eye.

12. Open your eyes and begin to mindfully notice the space around you. Lie in this position for several minutes breathing and reflecting on what you "saw" in your visualization meditation.

13. Incorporate crystals and gemstones to enhance the journey.

14. Try a yoga pose to bring you back into balance to achieve a higher state of awareness with your whole being.

15. Take a few deep inhales and exhales and move forward with your daily practice.

Creative visualization works wonders and is always useful in any meditation practice you incorporate into your healing path. Focusing on each energetic frequency, going through one at a time, will help you get better acquainted with all of the chakras individually so that you can balance them more effectively as a whole. Pursuit of the energetic balance you are looking for takes time and visualization is a fun and creative tool to help you understand and identify what is lurking under the surface and deep within your energy field.

All of the methods in this chapter are prescriptions for you to break through your chakra blocks and energetic imbalances to raise your vibrational frequency and live a happy, healthy and joyful life. You can use them on their own, or create your own, unique chakra healing rituals incorporating them altogether in one approach. The possibilities are endless and as you get more detailed with your healing work, and the more you cleanse and rebalance your energy, the better your intuition will be at knowing exactly what you need and when you need it.

Anything you take away from this chapter is to help you engage with a healing perspective and can be used in addition to any other healing practices you need to become balanced and whole. They are not intended to replace medical advice or professional guidance form a healthcare provider. All of these systems of healing can work well together to help you achieve your greatest health and most abundant life.

The final chapter of this book will help you to understand the best path forward to help you maintain regular daily balance with your chakra energy and lifestyle. It is all in your hands and you are the creator of your healing journey. The positive support outlined in this final chapter is intended to offer you motivation, guidance and tools to maintain a wholeness and happiness in all of your chakras.

Chapter 6: Maintaining Positive Vibrations

When you get to know yourself practically and energetically, you announce to yourself how you want to feel and who you are wanting to become. We are always going through some kind of growth and transformation process, even when we don't recognize that it is happening, and when you create awareness about this part of yourself, it is so much easier to maintain the lifestyle that works best for you and that feels the most whole and healthy.

With all of the knowledge that you have gained from this book so far, you can understand the quality of your vibrational frequency in a such way that you know what steps to take to heal the imbalances. The direction you take will be a surprise to you, because as you get going with this process, you will uncover unexpected mysteries deep within the layers of your being that are ready for focus and encouragement to heal.

The progress you make will always depend upon your interest in your growth and your choices to manifest the transformation you are desiring along the way. Progress can get halted, stumped, awkward, changeful, challenging and difficult. It can also flow smoothly, quietly, serenely, openly and refreshingly. It really just depends where you are in your healing process and how you work through the difficult moments that will help you align with your expansion.

When you are ready to fully unfold, your chakras will tell you how to guide and direct your healing. When you let go and let flow, you can really feel the guidance and support from yourself to do this challenging and opening work. What you will gain from this regular attention to your vibrational energy is a long life of holding your own, feeling charged and alive, expressing your true power and worth, letting love grow with you as you grow, and feeling your intuition thrive through all life matters as you move forward.

The next sections are ready to provide you with all of the ongoing tools for support that you will need to stay in focused concentration with your energetic healing and chakra rebalancing. These methods and tools are simple and practical, and with regular practice, they will inform your life experience in new and expansive ways. The places that you will travel within your own world of light is an exciting discovery process and should be regarded as a profoundly personal and magical journey like no other you have known.

Practicing Self-Love

There are many ways that people practice self-love, but what does that even mean and how will that help your chakras? If you have learned anything from this book, then you know that energy is manifested through the emotions and that when we are experiencing "love energy" we are at a higher vibrational frequency. This frequency is what heals people when they are sick, calms them when they are distressed, and makes them feel like everything is going to be okay.

Love vibrations are a specific frequency and can correct a lot of negative energy, stimulating a rebalancing of the chakras that might be blocked or problematic. All of the energy in your heart chakra wants to vibrate at the love frequency and is looking for healing in this area the most.

When you have an open-heart chakra, you are engaging in a high vibration of energy that will impact all of the other chakras to a great degree and will help you connect more deeply and compassionately to your healing journey. It can be a hard experience, to heal the wounds of the heart, and when you do, you will do it through loving yourself the most.

Some people might get concerned about being too narcissistic or egotistical about loving themselves, however, self-love was never meant to be considered something that would be construed as negative, as narcissism and egomania are; self-love is a form of healthy and balanced ego of the self and revolves around loving others as well. When you are able to love yourself all the way, you are passively enjoying the love of all beings on Earth, and you are better able to offer your love in return.

The connection between the heart chakra and the palms is very strong. You have thousands of nerves and receptors in your hands that can communicate with your brain in a variety of ways. Touch is one of our most powerful senses and informs a lot of our energetic experiences. Your hands also have powerful energy centers in the palms and can feel in this way, too.

You can shift the energy of your heart simply by placing your hand over this chakra and taking several deep breaths. Try the following Self-Love Heart Chakra Meditation to help you see what it can do to your overall energy:

Self-Love Heart Chakra Meditation

1. Sit in a comfortable position and close your eyes.

2. Bring your focus to your breath and take several deep inhales in and exhales out.

3. Bring both hands to your heart chakra and lay them over your heart, one on top of the other, palms down.

4. Sit in this pose for several moments and continue to breathe deeply.

5. Visualize the green energy of the heart chakra widening and opening to receive the gift of your love. Let yourself smile as you soften your face and jaw.

6. Focus on your thoughts and let anything negative be washed away and released.

7. Think, or say aloud the following mantra:

   "I am ready to receive love from myself. I am worthy of love from myself. I am a good and kind person and I feel open to loving who I am and what I want in this world. I am okay with letting go of any negative thoughts and ideas I have about myself. I am okay with taking on the responsibility of loving myself well. I have a lot of love to give and I give it to myself now."

8. You can change the words to be more specific to you and who you are, or you can use only one of these sentences and repeat it over and over again. It is up to you.

9. Sit in repose for several moments with your hands moved to your lap and just relax with a feeling of calm and an open heart.

10. Gently open your eyes and keep your loving vibration with you. You can repeat this meditation any time you begin to doubt yourself or start thinking or saying negative words or ideas about yourself.

The purpose of self-love in all of this is that you align more frequently with the frequency of love and the energy of that vibration to help you stay focused on your healing path. It is remarkable how effective healthy self-love practices can be, and a lot of those practices include some of the chakra healing methods you have already learned in this book.

Take a look at this list of sample ideas for how to practice self-love on a regular, every day basis (and you do want to practice self-love every single day for your own benefit and healing):

- Practice healing physical exercise, such as Yoga, dance, swimming, walking, cycling, etc.

- Feed yourself well (i.e., lay off the junk and eat a balanced meal).

- Practice meditation and mindfulness.
- Offer yourself a gift of some kind (you don't have to buy yourself something every day; the gift could be to watch your favorite movie at the end of the day, or go to your favorite park and have a relaxing picnic. It can also be

an object you have been wanting to get, or splurging on a fancy ice cream cone).

- Get good rest and put yourself to bed at a reasonable hour.

- Practice loving affirmation and meditation (see Self-Love Heart Chakra Meditation)

- Take the trip you have always wanted to take and set aside time to save money for it.

- Enjoy soothing and relaxing baths by candlelight.

- Take yourself out on a date; get dressed up and treat yourself to a beautiful night at your favorite restaurant.

- Spend time lovingly caressing yourself and feeling your own loving touch.

- Create healthy boundaries with other people and situations in your life that counteract your self-love practices.

- Begin to seek out the career that means the most to you and is more of what you have always wanted.

- Celebrate your successes AND your failures with good experiences and occasions (Note** Our "failures" and mistakes are equally as important as our success. They are how we learn and teach ourselves to get better and should be equally celebrated as a way to break new ground and find out more of where we are wanting to go).

- Teach yourself something you have always wanted to learn.

These are only a few examples of how to practice self-love, and you may have a few ideas already of how you want to engage with that in your own way. Make it a daily ritual and let it become your regular starting point every day. If you feel like you are out of love with yourself, you can easily get back to that energy and frequency by reminding yourself with the Self-Love Heart Chakra meditation outlined in this chapter.

Balance and Harmony

Connecting to your heart energy will have a huge impact on your healing journey and will help you maintain an equilibrium of "everything will be okay and I am good at taking care of my needs". Once you get going with chakra healing work, you open up a whole lot of different kinds of cans of worms that need to be addressed and understood. This can be an emotional time and you may feel inclined to reject a lot of your feelings or experiences and can end up reverting back to old habits and patterns that feel more "comfortable".

The truth is, your only comfortable in those realities because you had to teach yourself to live that way (ex: always avoiding confrontation at the expense of your own feelings; choosing the bottle of red wine over water and a good night's sleep; telling yourself you will never get that promotion, over and over again). As much as you have learned how to live your life with certain behaviors, thoughts and ideas, you can unlearn them by teaching yourself new ways to balance and harmonize your energy to reflect more of your true nature.

What is true nature and how do you find that out? If you are ever struggling and fighting against yourself (and even others: projection), you will be acting against what you are truly wanting for yourself. If you are working in a career that drains your energy and makes you feel unhappy, then you are not in the right career for yourself. If you are uncomfortable staying married to someone who causes you to doubt how you like to be, then you are likely not in the right relationship for you. If you are struggling to stay focused on what it is that you are truly wanting to do with your life, it is because you are listening to your fears that it won't be possible.

Finding balance and harmony with yourself means that you have to work everyday to understand what your attitude toward your life and yourself is, and how to maintain that philosophy and energy. Through the healing process of working with your chakras, you will uncover so much of these truths about who you are, what you want the most, and what is likely standing in your path to getting there.

Finding harmony and balance in those times can feel like a chore and your energy and attitude to your growth is what will help you continue moving forward. The best ways to achieve harmony and balance are to work with the energy of opposites. Here is an example of what that means:

- You are angry and frustrated and can't seem to smooth your feathers after weeks of feeling stuck in a rut with your chakra healing practices. You are engaging with all of the methods that were shown to you and you still have made any breakthroughs. You feel unsure of what to do next and so you allow yourself to feel painful and uneasy about what you are doing, rejecting the goals you had in mind, and the process you are going through

- To regain harmony and balance, consider the energy that you are holding onto. It is saying that you can't do this and that you will never figure out how to heal like this, or that you should just quit because you can't see any big differences or changes. If you have these feelings come up, they are asking you to shift your ideas and look for alternative voice inside of yourself to inform your progress. The harmony and balance that you can regain comes from teaching yourself how to effectively process this type of feeling.

- To reassure yourself that you are doing well, you can alter your perception of the situation by contemplating your emotions and why they are happening in the first place. Did you have an immediate result in mind? Do you plan on your healing only taking a certain amount of time? Are you eager to change and therefore frustrated because you have noticed any major shifts? Are you able to recognize that the very feelings you are having pertain to growth and that you are making progress, right in this moment?

- Harmony and balance require reflection and contemplation. To achieve this state of being, you have to question your position, your feelings, your experiences.

It may seem too simple, but the truth is, you will always fluctuate back and forth until you have learned how to understand you own energetic processes. When something is feeling negative, look for how it is positive (opposites). It isn't hard to find the patterns, once you really begin to pay attention. Once you identify the patterns you create with your emotions and energies, then you will know how to change them, thus regaining balance and harmony.

Be patient with yourself and act from a curiosity rather than a judgement of yourself. You can always find better inner harmony when you are inquisitive instead of accusatory.

Applications for Everyday

Your everyday chakra healing practice is already all laid out for you in this book. Each chapter has given you all of the knowledge, understanding and tools you need to begin this momentous journey. There are places for you to dig deeply into yourself and uncover your beautiful truths, buried underneath the layers of energetic blockages and imbalances. What is lurking under there? Are you ready to look?

To help you give focus to your healing path with your chakras, here is a list of everyday applications to keep you in focus and practice:

1. Begin your day with a meditation and some yoga instead of 3 cups of coffee.

2. Spend time in the morning sun with your journal and time for reflection.

3. Practice mindfulness on your way to work.

4. Take a meditation break at the office.

5. Carry your preferred chakra healing crystals with you so you can feel energetically harmonious.

6. Take time in your day to check in with your feelings and your physical body. As yourself if you have tension anywhere, or what kinds of thoughts are you focusing on?

7. Visit a place that has meaning for you.

8. Practice a self-love meditation.

9. At the end of your day, determine where you are feeling the most "off" and perform a chakra healing meditation to get you back in balance.

10. Eat a healthy meal and have a relaxing evening with friends and/or family.

11. Get a good night's sleep.

12. Take good care of your body by listening to it when it is shouting out to you that something is off.

13. Enjoy some indulgences every once and a while.

14. Find a moment in your day to dance or sing.

15. Share your feelings with a friend, colleague or partner.

16. Offer yourself time to do something creative.

17. Do something you have been afraid to try.

18. Spend time in nature.

19. Spend time in water (baths, swimming, etc.)

20. Devote time to yourself alone.

21. Record your experiences and keep a diary of your progress.

22. Listen to your words as they come up for acknowledgement in your mind and discover what your mind is telling you; where does it lead (which chakra)?

There are so many ways to look for healing and opening in your energy centers. These applications are only the beginning of how to start helping your energy shift every day. The more you practice understanding your energy, the easier it becomes to listen and respond to what you are really needing, wanting, and asking to remove and rebalance.

Look for ways to enjoy these applications in your own life, or find some that are not listed here that really work for you. Your journey is in your hands and your energy is ready to vibrate at a higher frequency. Practice self-love, bring balance and harmony back into your life, and do it every day!

Conclusion

Congratulations on your journey through the chakras and learning all you need to know about how to begin healing your own energy! This book is a welcoming resource for you to start practicing the healing process and with all of your new knowledge about chakras, you can begin to explore in a more in-depth way on your own. Your intuition is all you need now, to help you achieve the level of balance and vibrational flow required to feel that wholeness and enlightenment that comes from an unblocked and healthy chakra system.

This book has shown you the beautiful history and discovery of the chakras as well as an understanding of how we can use modern science to explore and explain what is really happening on the energetic level with our bodies. The connection between the chakras and the physical/emotional self is strong and I hope that you can now see how dynamic our total being truly is within that mind-body-spirit balance.

You have taken a unique road trip through the chakra system and learned about how each of them has distinct qualities and characteristics that set them apart from each other, and how all together, they create a uniform wholeness that leads to the transcendent self and connection to the truth and purpose of your life.

All of the information in this book is here to show you what kinds of ailments, issues and challenges can present themselves when your chakras are unhealthy, blocked and imbalanced. As you move forward, you can begin to identify these causes and side-effects in your own life and begin to energetically treat yourself through the healing process.

You have all of the techniques outlined for you to get started and any number of them will shift and transform your energy the more you practice them. Remember that daily or weekly energy clearing, using any of these methods, will keep you in a better balance overall.

The goal of this book is to show you how to work with your chakra energy for a fuller, happier, healthier life and how-to bring positivity into your vibration and frequency more regularly. The power of living in balance will bring into you harmony with the life you have always wanted to live. Moving forward, keep your energy open and flowing using these chakra healing techniques and the knowledge you have gained about your own, unique energy system.

Everything that you do in your life, and every person you encounter, will influence your energy and your chakras. We carry this energy around with us, sometimes for our whole lives and if you are wanting to heal the wounds of the past, traumatic circumstances, chronic health problems, emotional challenges and upheaval, to create a more balanced and energetically vibrant life, then all you have to do is listen to your energy and "read" your chakras.

Refer to this book as often as you need to in order to stay focused on your healing path. You can use it as a platform to get you started and to lead you into even deeper knowledge about how all of your chakras work to balance each other out. Bring this knowledge into your every day self-care routines and practices and watch your life transform.

I hope that you have found this book informative and enlightening and if you feel it has helped you on your path to healing in any way, a review on Amazon.com is always appreciated! Thank you for reading and may your energy flow freely!

Made in United States
North Haven, CT
24 September 2022

24495041R00078